OUT

OF

DARKNESS:

FAITH, PATIENCE, AND HIS PROMISES

by

RYAN JAMES FOSTER

Religion & Spirituality

Spiritual Formation

© 2026 Ryan James Foster

All rights reserved.

ISBN: 979-8-9952644-0-8

TABLE OF CONTENTS

DISCLAIMER

Although this book is designed to provide accurate information regarding the subject matter covered, the publisher and the author assume no responsibility for errors, inaccuracies, omissions, or any inconsistencies herein. This book is meant as a source of valuable information for the reader, however, it is not meant as a replacement for direct expert assistance. If such a level of assistance is required, the services of a competent professional should be sought. If you or a loved one are suicidal connect with help using the number 988.

DEDICATION

To Kerri, my rock and my heart, your love and strength have carried me through the darkest times. Thank you for never giving up on me, even when I couldn't see the way out. You are my constant reminder of grace and faith.

And to Adeline, my beautiful daughter, you are the light that shines bright in my life. Your innocence and joy remind me daily of the reasons to keep going. This journey is as much for you as it is for me.

With all my love.

13 And Moses said to the people, "Fear not, stand firm, and see the salvation of the Lord, which he will work for you today. For the Egyptians whom you see today, you shall never see again. 14 The Lord will fight for you, and you have only to be silent."

Exodus 14:13-14 English Standard Version

PREFACE

Depression is more than a word, it's a battle between life and death. Its weight is crushing, its darkness suffocating. And yet, I share my story. In these pages, you will walk with me through the pit of hell that depression is, and witness the highs, the lows, and the unthinkable in-between moments that shaped my journey. You will see me at my most vulnerable, facing the raw and unfiltered reality of what it means to fight for survival when every part of you wants to give up. But you will also see God's faithfulness in the midst of my deepest despair; how He walked with me and helped me climb out of the darkness.

I wrote this book not only to tell my story but to stand as a voice for those silently fighting their own battles with depression. My hope is that through my experiences, others will find a voice, a lifeline, and the courage to keep fighting. I know what it feels like to stare into the pit, unsure if I would make it out alive. I understand the hopelessness, the numbness, and the lies depression whispers. That's why I want to say to you, honestly, you are not alone. There is a way out, even when you can't see it.

In these chapters, I will share what I learned on this journey. Lessons about myself, resilience, and the importance of seeking help from God. If you or someone you know is struggling with suicidal thoughts, please don't wait. Reach out. You are worth saving. Call or text 988, the Suicide and Crisis Lifeline, to speak with someone who can help. There is no shame in asking for help; in fact, it may be your most courageous step.

As you turn the page to Chapter 1, I'll take you back to the night when everything shifted. The night I was suddenly thrust into the depths of depression. That moment marked the beginning of a fight I wasn't sure I could win. But by God's grace, here I stand. And so can you.

CHAPTER 1

June 10, 2021:

The Day My World Was Shattered

June 10, 2021. I can only describe it now as a day from the pits of hell, a day of darkness. It is a day I will never forget, though I wish I could. When that morning began, those words would never have crossed my mind. It started as an ordinary day, giving no hint of the terrible storm that was about to consume me.

Until then, my life had been incredibly fortunate, overflowing with blessings. I grew up with two loving parents in the farm country of west-central Indiana. I was born on a cool fall afternoon just across the state line in Danville, Illinois, at Parkview Hospital. Though I was extremely jaundiced, I was otherwise a healthy baby.

I was raised in Wallace, Indiana, a tiny town in Fountain County, a map dot with barely a hundred people, and shrinking. Wallace had no stoplights, only a handful of stop signs. Founded in the 1830s, it was once called Jackville. It wasn't known for much, though we did have a Miss Indiana State Fair Queen come from Wallace. That was a big deal. The town even put up a sign to celebrate it.

My childhood home sat just outside the town square, surrounded by open land with lush Kentucky bluegrass and a green forest in the backyard, where Stillwater Creek wound its way through. It was country living at its finest.

Even though we lived just beyond the square, Wallace was always at the center of our lives. On Sundays, we went to the little white Wallace Christian Church. I can still see myself sitting in a pew, singing hymns like How Great Thou Art and Wonderful Words of Life as the preacher spoke about Jesus.

We spent much of the week in town, too. My parents owned Foster's General Store, right downtown across from the post office and the Masonic Lodge. Both buildings are gone now, torn down and replaced by the town hall.

When you hear the phrase general store, what do you picture? You're probably right. Foster's General Store had everything from candy and lunch meats to nuts, bolts, and even belts for your car engine. Farmers gathered around the round table with coffee, and some ordered biscuits and gravy. Their conversations drifted from the weather and crops to the Hoosiers and the Boilermakers. I loved sitting there, listening to every word. Sometimes I thought, Maybe I'll be a farmer one day. Around that table, you could learn just about anything from how tractor hydraulics worked to who was the better coach: Bobby Knight or Gene Keady.

I grew up with parents who loved me deeply. They gave me everything I needed and more. We went on countless vacations.

I remember Yellowstone National Park, where we saw Old Faithful, the bison, and winding mountain roads. At the end of the trip, they bought me a bright yellow Yogi Bear shirt I adored. We also took plenty of road trips closer to home. My dad loved '50s and '60s music and never missed Solid Gold Saturday Night. I grew up with the oldies on the radio, enjoying songs like Pretty Woman by Roy Orbison and It's My Party by Lesley Gore. Even today, those songs spark a wave of nostalgia.

I also had a sister, four years older, and we shared a strong brother-sister bond. Many afternoons we roller-skated in the basement to Kylie Minogue's Locomotion and other '80s hits. To this day, I don't care much for '80s music, maybe that's why. Summers were spent on our ten-speed bikes, riding loops through the backyard, down the gravel road, and past cornfields and woods. I remember the corn swaying in the breeze while gravel dust lingered in the air. Eventually, the road in front of our house was paved, thanks to my parents and neighbors pooling together.

Our neighbors weren't close in proximity, but they were remarkable people. One, who lived a quarter mile away, won a million dollars on the Hoosier Lottery show. Another, half a mile away, invented a guttering system. Despite the distance, I liked the isolation.

My dad worked tirelessly to give us everything and more. He taught us how to raise livestock, which became a big part of my life. We had show steers and barrows, along with show rabbits. My mother lived for my sister and me. I don't just believe she would have died for us, I know she would have. We were her everything. I'm not sure that kind of devotion was healthy, but we always knew she loved us. I may not have recognized it back then, but now I see it clearly.

Looking back, I realize how much I loved that place, the country and the freedom it gave me. The cornfields in the summer. The deer nibbling from the locust tree in the backyard. The clear, shallow creek running through the woods behind the house. I grew up in the same home my parents still live in today, a modest abode tucked away in the middle of nowhere. I spent countless days wandering the woods and wading in the creek. Summer nights were unforgettable, with the cool breeze sweeping through and lightning bugs flickering in the darkness.

Some of my best memories come from the Fountain County 4-H Fair. Every July, for ten years straight, I poured myself into project after project. It was my life. I especially loved showing livestock, with cattle being my favorite. Each summer I came home with purple ribbon after purple ribbon. Grand Champion, that was the goal, and I was on fire. I lived for those wins.

I'll never forget one year when I won Grand Champion for my Tractor Poster. Instead of a trophy, I received a big flashlight. I was crushed. I remember running off stage in tears, bawling my eyes out. Winning wasn't just about recognition, it was about the trophies. Still, I kept winning: Floral Arrangement, Garden, Horseless Horse, and more. My room filled with trophies lined along the shelves, each one a reminder of my determination. And then, sitting among them all, was that one oversized flashlight.

Life was so good then, not perfect, but good and full of favor. Even so, I've spent years analyzing my past, searching for the seed of my depression, trying to understand what could have led to that horrible day.

As a kid, I was pretty unsocial. I liked school, but I wasn't interested in making a lot of friends. I had my small circle, and that was enough. My connection at school came through sports. I was an athlete, competing all three seasons of the year   cross country, swimming, and track. A three-season varsity letterman. I was good at it, and I loved winning.

Academically, school was easy for me. Most classes were a breeze and didn't require much studying. The only one that caught me off guard was Algebra II Honors. My cousin was the teacher, which didn't help. I didn't want to ask him questions or admit I was struggling. After talking with the guidance counselor, I realized I could drop down to regular Algebra II and still graduate with an Academic Honors Diploma. My cross-country coach taught that class, and it turned out to be simple. Still, it felt strange. In a small school like mine, everyone in my grade was in the Honors class, while most of the students in my new class seemed remedial. I was also the youngest in the room.

I graduated with a class of just 100 students. The elementary school was right across the parking lot from the Junior-Senior High, so I knew everyone, the students, the teachers, the staff. My father was on the school board, which meant everyone knew me, too. That didn't always work in my favor.

Sometimes, I let it go to my head. I remember one day in World History class, my teacher made me stand up and scolded me in front of everyone. He said, "I don't care if your dad is the president of the School Board, you are obnoxious." All I could do was sit back down.

Another time, when I was an office aide, I clashed with one of the high school secretaries. She was notoriously rude, especially to people she didn't like or didn't think were good enough. One day, I saw her being disrespectful to a family that came in. Without thinking, I walked right up to her and said, "You're rude, and you shouldn't even do this job." Should I have said that? No way. But I did.

The principal called me in afterward and asked if I'd be willing to apologize to her. "Absolutely not," I said, and walked away. I'm still working on that attitude to this day.

In school, I was bullied, but who wasn't? My bully was Kevin. He was a grade older than me, and he was such a jerk. I should have punched him when I had the chance, but I wasn't a violent guy. Looking back, I realize that most bullies are dealing with their own issues. I don't know if it was depression or something else, but Kevin clearly had problems.

Despite that, I don't remember ever feeling depressed as a teenager. Still, my family went through some traumatic experiences that tugged at the edges of my seemingly wonderful life. People say trauma can leave lasting marks, and I believe that.

When I was eight, my mom was diagnosed with a brain tumor. At the time, I didn't fully understand what that meant. Now, as an adult, I realize how terrified my parents must have been. Brain surgery is no small thing; she could have died or been left paralyzed.

One night, my mom sat us down and explained the risks of her upcoming surgery. She told us there was a chance she might not survive, or that she might come out "a vegetable." Those were her exact words. I didn't really understand, but I knew it wasn't good. I still remember standing in the basement by the washer and dryer as my mom showed me how to do laundry just in case she didn't make it. She said, "Someone will have to do the laundry." Lord, what a thought to carry at eight years old.

Another dramatic event happened when I was a freshman in high school. My sister had just started her freshman year at the University of Southern Indiana. She was a Delta Zeta, which I thought was the coolest thing. USI seemed like a dream school to me, and I wanted to go there one day. But for her, it turned into a nightmare.

One late night, my parents got a phone call that jolted the whole house awake. Back then, we had a landline, so whenever someone called, every phone in the house rang at once. I don't remember the exact time, only that it was the middle of the night, pitch black outside, and I'd been sleeping just before the phone rang.

All I remember is sitting up in bed, listening to the panic and despair in my mom's voice as she spoke on the phone. I couldn't hear the other side of the conversation. To this day, I still don't know who she was talking to, maybe a police officer, maybe someone at the hospital.

At the time, my sister was working a late-night job as a telemarketer. I'm not sure why   maybe she wanted to earn her own money, maybe she just wanted independence. That night, after finishing her shift, she drove her little red Pontiac back to the Delta Zeta house and parked in the dimly lit lot behind the building.

As she was getting out of her car, a man in a black ski mask approached her on foot and pulled a gun. He forced her back into the car and ordered her to drive to a remote area outside of Evansville, in Mount Vernon, Indiana. There, he held her at gunpoint and forced her into an empty livestock trailer.

That night, my parents were told over the phone that my sister had been kidnapped and raped. The rest of that story is hers to tell, not mine. But the event marked the beginning of a long, difficult year for my sister, my parents, and even me. I don't think my parents realized that I was awake and absorbing half of that late-night conversation as I sat frozen in bed.

The memory after that phone call is blurry. I think I remember them waking me up to explain what had happened and to let me know that my dad was leaving immediately to drive to Evansville. The following 365 days were some of the hardest of our lives. My dad and sister were able to hide their emotions, but my mom couldn't.

My sister had to endure the trial of her attacker in Vanderburgh County. We spent weeks in Evansville as the trial unfolded, staying at the Fairfield Inn off Highway 41. For me, that hotel became a strange safe place in the middle of so much darkness.

Every day, my parents and I sat in the courtroom, listening to witness after witness take the stand. The day my sister testified was the hardest for my mom. When the jury returned with a verdict, I remember my mom whispering that she was going to be sick. My dad told her she had to stay. It would look bad if she left.

Justice was eventually served: the rapist was found guilty of kidnapping with a deadly weapon and of rape. But the entire ordeal broke my mom in ways that time never truly healed. This scar has stayed with her, and with all of us, ever since.

I know my mom has never gotten over it. The memory still haunts her, and it comes up even now. Every year, she wrote letters to fight against the rapist's possible parole. When the man who assaulted my sister finally served his time and was released, it nearly broke her. She even told us she wanted to meet him at the prison gates and deliver her own final sentence. That never happened, praise God. But not long after, that awful man kidnapped and raped another woman. He's back in prison now, this time for much longer.

For a while, I told myself that terrible things just happen to families. Still, even in the middle of so much darkness, I felt favor resting on me. Yet sometimes I wonder if that was simply another step toward my eventual breakdown.

That same sense of favor followed me when I moved to Bloomington, Indiana, to attend Indiana University. I had wanted to go to IU for as long as I could remember, and I absolutely loved the campus and the town. It was only a two-hour drive from my parents' house, far enough to feel independent, but close enough that I could return whenever I needed their comfort or just wanted to drop off a bag of laundry.

I never once did laundry on campus. I either took it to the dry cleaners or carried duffle bags home for my mom to handle. College life felt like it was made for me. I met wonderful people during my four years there, and IU Hoosier basketball became one of my greatest joys. I attended every home game, wearing my cream-and-crimson sweatshirt and shouting, "Go IU, fight, fight, fight!"

Eventually, I declared my major in Elementary Education. In hindsight, it seems inevitable. I had always wanted to be a teacher. Some of my earliest memories are of "playing school" as a child, standing at my whiteboard, teaching imaginary students with those strong-smelling Expo markers. I loved that smell. They don't make them like that anymore. Becoming an education major just made sense, and I flourished at IU, making the most of living on my own for the first time.

But looking back, I can also see the cracks forming. I began to slip away from the beliefs I had held as a Christian. I started doing things I knew weren't good for me. In Bloomington, I stopped going to church altogether. In fact, during all four years at IU, I didn't attend once in that city. Now that it's behind me, I'm not proud of that.

When I went home to Wallace, though, I still went to church with my parents. Sometimes I even played the hymns on piano if Cindy, our pianist, couldn't be there. I still own that old hymnal, sitting on my piano today.

I could pound out Amazing Grace or The Old Rugged Cross on those ivory keys like the best of them. But in Bloomington, I also loved cutting loose. My nights often revolved around whichever bar had the best drink special: Margarita Mondays at Tumbleweed, Tuesdays at Yogi's for Long Islands and mini corn dogs, Wednesdays at the Bluebird for 25-cent drafts, and Thursdays through Saturdays at Sports, where the DJ kept the music going until two in the morning.

I drank a lot during those years and made more than my share of bad choices. Looking back, maybe that's where my struggle with alcohol first began, a road that eventually led to that dreadful day in June. Still, even in my recklessness, God's hand was on me. I did things I shouldn't have, but by His grace, I made it through.

My life overflowed with favor, and even though I drifted from the Lord for a time, He never drifted from me. Why did I forget that during my breakdown?

After my time as a Hoosier, I moved to the Sunshine State. Never in a million years did I imagine leaving Indiana, 1,001 miles away from home. That long thousand miles broke my mom's heart when I told her I was going south. Yet in Florida, blessings waited for me.

I began my career in education, teaching fourth grade at Socrum Elementary in Lakeland. It was an exciting place to work, and I learned so much, not only about teaching, but about myself. Teaching was hard. At times, I wanted to quit, but I was determined not to fail. I refused to move back to Indiana and face the question: What happened in Florida?

Even then, I don't remember signs of depression, but I do recognize the early shadows of alcoholism. Before I met Kerri, I had a few friends, but I was often alone. After all, I had moved to Florida completely on my own.

A typical Friday or Saturday night back then was just me, my Bose SoundDock and iPod, a large Hungry Howie's pizza, and a bottle of champagne. I'd eat, drink, and play music until I eventually fell asleep. Hardly the highlight of my life.

Still, the brightest thing to come out of Socrum was meeting my wife. We both started teaching there in the fall of 2005. I'd drop off my fourth graders at their special-area class just as she was supposed to be picking up her second graders. She was late almost every day, which meant I had to keep an eye on her class. She'll deny it, but I know it's true.

We lived in the same apartment complex, Audubon Oaks, and eventually decided to carpool. Before long, we started dating. That courtship was one of the best times of my life. I had never dated a woman like her, truthfully, I'd never been in a serious relationship before. There was something undeniably different about her. Her kindness and love for people was unlike anything I had ever known.

We dated for almost three years, and I wasn't sure what came next. I had never loved anyone like this, and I wasn't sure what the next step should be. Then, one July afternoon while we sat in my parents' living room in Indiana, she looked at me and asked, "Where are we going with this?" It wasn't an easy conversation, it was one of those moments where you either move forward or walk away. I can't remember what I said, but I know the message was clear: it was time to take the next step.

A month later, in August, I proposed to her at my favorite restaurant in Lakeland, The Terrace Grille. I had arranged for the staff to place the ring inside a flower on a dessert. I was a nervous wreck, barely able to remember what we ate that night. When the waitress asked if we wanted dessert, Kerri said no, of course, she was full. My heart sank, and I quickly jumped in: "Actually, yes, I'd like dessert." Eventually, the dessert arrived, and so did the question I had been waiting to ask.

She said yes. I was a nervous wreck, but it became one of the most incredible memories of my life. We spent the next year planning our wedding. When the day finally came, so many of our guests were from Socrum Elementary, that little school where everything began.

Our June wedding in the sweltering summer of 2009 was lavish yet intimate, filled with family, friends, and joy. We said our vows outdoors on a farm, an absolutely perfect setting for me. It was beautiful, one of the happiest days I can remember. At that time, there were still no signs of depression in my life. I had even stopped drinking, and it didn't feel like a struggle anymore.

Marriage was wonderful for us. Our home was filled with peace, joy, and laughter. After our wedding, we lived life to the fullest, traveling, exploring, and building a future together. As our 12th wedding anniversary approached, just three days away when the fog of despair finally settled over me. Life seemed solid and secure. My wife had been my constant support and closest companion. We rarely fought in all those years of marriage; in fact, I can only recall two arguments, both of which involved curry. To this day, we still joke about avoiding curry in our house.

My marriage was everything I never knew I wanted. I had a beautiful wife, a fulfilling life, and eventually, a daughter who was born just three years before my breakdown. She brought warmth, sparkle, and delight into our days. Life was grand.

But looking back now, I wonder if I was quietly struggling. Fatherhood didn't come naturally to me. I wanted to be a supportive husband and a good dad, but I wasn't sure I was getting it right. Maybe the seeds of depression were already planted, creeping closer without me realizing it.

During the last month of Kerri's pregnancy, we were also house-hunting. The very day our daughter was born, we received an offer on the house we were selling. When we moved into a recovery room at the hospital with our newborn, I finally checked my phone and told Kerri, "Hey, we got an offer on our house." The buyer wanted to close in two weeks. We asked for four.

My in-laws helped pack us up while we deliriously tried to care for a newborn who was jaundiced and losing weight. For the first week of her life, we were at the doctor's office every single day. At the same time, we had no home of our own, so we moved in with my in-laws. We told them it would be just for two months. It turned into two years while we searched for the perfect place to call home.

During that season, I also had a job I loved to hate. I was a leader at a school overshadowed by a heavy, almost tangible darkness. Not everyone was consumed by it. Some faithful Christians would gather to pray over the campus, but the oppression there weighed heavily on me. That story could fill an entire book of its own.

Balancing the emotions of caring for a newborn daughter, living with my in-laws, searching for a house, and working in such an oppressive environment was anything but easy. Looking back, I wonder if all that stress was the first warning sign of my impending breakdown.

By the time everything finally collapsed, those struggles were already resolved. We had found our dream home and even appeared on an episode of House Hunters. (It was heavily edited; you'll have to see it for yourself.) The family was thriving, and we loved our new house. On top of that, I had stepped into a new job that not only provided financial stability but also gave me professional fulfillment and opportunities for growth.

From the outside, my life looked incredibly rich with love, purpose, and blessings. But deep down, there were cracks. In hindsight, I can see the subtle signs of anxiety, depression, and perhaps another disorder slowly creeping in. I never realized how close the darkness was, or how the evil I had been outrunning would eventually catch up to me, knocking me off my feet and leaving me broken.

Little did I know, as I walked into the grand Caribe Royale Hotel in Orlando that dreaded week of June, my life was about to take a devastating turn that would plunge me into years of pain and suffering.

The memory of that moment on June 10, 2021, remains etched in my mind vivid, haunting, unforgettable. It was a balmy afternoon in Florida, the air heavy with the anticipation of summer. If you've ever been to Florida in June, you can almost feel the humidity pressing against your skin and the heat rising from the pavement as you read this.

I was attending a professional conference for an association my wife and I both belonged to through our careers. Traveling together was always a blessing, a shared perk of our work. We were staying at the beautiful Caribe Royale Resort, a place designed for rest and escape, with its sparkling blue pool, rock cave, and fast water slide. Disney World and the other parks were only a short drive away. My wife and I felt blessed to steal away some quality time before a friend brought our daughter to join us.

Quality time has always been my love language, so by all accounts I should have been on cloud nine. The hotel lobby pulsed with the chatter of guests, their laughter weaving through the soft notes of a piano in the background. I remember wondering, was that Chopin? The atmosphere was vibrant, alive, the kind of setting that should have filled me with wonder and delight. Instead, a dreadful shadow crept in, veiling my spirit.

I remember the exact instant it struck. A heavy cloud seemed to descend without warning, draining every ounce of joy from me, joy that would not return for years. The memory is seared into me, clear as daylight even now.

I was sitting on one of the queen beds in our suite, just behind my family. My wife, daughter, and friend moved busily around the room, getting ready for the evening. I had just finished a productive day at the conference, showered, and dressed for the 1920s-themed party that night. They were still preparing, curling hair, applying makeup, and laughing softly. My wife was carefully braiding our daughter's hair, some intricate design I can still picture.

And there I sat, staring into the mirror. Looking too deeply. Looking past my reflection into something I didn't yet understand.

I wasn't sure what I was staring at, but I couldn't pull my eyes from the mirror. We always dressed to the nines for theme parties, and this night was no exception. As a family, we had coordinated our costumes with care. My daughter sparkled in a black sequined dress trimmed with gold fringe, my wife looked radiant in a black sequined cocktail dress, and I wore a sharp suit topped with a classic 1920s hat. Dressing up for these moments had always brought me joy. This time, it should have.

But instead, a wave of darkness slammed into me. A fog, thick and suffocating, crashed across my mind. I tried to go about the moment, to interact, to play the role of myself. Yet I could not think clearly. I could not function like a normal human being.

It felt as if I had become someone else entirely. In less than a second, nearly forty years of familiarity with myself dissolved. The sensation was like a heavy fishing net hurled over me, dragging me to the ground, leaving me thrashing and gasping for air. My hands clawed at invisible binds, my breath caught in my throat. It was as if I'd been hurled into an alternate universe where nothing felt stable or real.

Did anyone notice? Could they see something was wrong? Or was I masking it well enough?

Even now, I struggle to put words to the emotions of that moment. They were ordinary feelings of anger, sadness, jealousy, and fear, but twisted together in a violent remix that felt wholly unnatural. A concoction not of this world, but from the very pits of hell.

I didn't yet know what was happening to me. But I did know this: life would never be the same again.

Looking back now, I can see that the wave of depression had been creeping toward me for some time, inching closer day by day. Yet its arrival was anything but gradual. It struck with ruthless force, like a sudden storm breaking over the calm sea of my life. In an instant, the joy that once colored my world was swept away, leaving me stranded on an empty, desolate shore. Alone.

When depression crashes over you, it is overwhelming, disorienting, and suffocating. The weight of sadness makes you painfully aware of the darkness consuming your thoughts. In those depths, reaching out feels impossible. Even the idea that someone might understand seems foreign. So I hid it. I hid it from everyone, even from my wife. It was nearly impossible. She could see something was wrong   but my attempts at masking only made me seem distant, even irrational. To her, I probably looked crazy. To me, I felt utterly abandoned.

The loneliness magnified everything. In that exact moment it hit, I was convinced everyone was against me and that life itself was against me. How could I possibly go on like this?

At the time, I didn't recognize it for what it was. I couldn't name the weight crushing me or trace the source of my anguish. I only knew I had lost all joy, replaced by a constant churn of irritation, insecurity, and sadness. And woven into that storm was jealousy. It was fierce, irrational, and consuming. Its intensity bewildered me. I didn't yet understand that it was only a symptom, a mask for the deeper depression I had been running from.

One evening during the conference, my wife invited me to dinner with her colleagues at the Columbia Restaurant. It should have been a beautiful night, good food, good company, a chance to enjoy being together. Instead, I seethed with jealousy and resentment. That night, what should have been lovely became another reminder that something inside me was unraveling.

The tapas were being passed and the famous "1905" salad was shared around the table. I sat at the far end, isolated in plain sight, sinking deeper into whatever darkness had hold of me. My wife hardly acknowledged me, which only sharpened the ache.

At one point, I reached for her drink. The woman beside her gave me a strange look and said, "Uh, that man is drinking your drink." A woman two seats away didn't even realize we were married. The sting of invisibility lit my chest on fire.

I could feel the anger coursing through my veins, hot, unfamiliar, uncontrollable. I latched onto the easiest explanation: It's her fault. She's ignoring me. Blaming her gave me something to hold onto, a reason for the rage. But deep down, I knew it wasn't true. The resentment was just another symptom of what was really happening inside me, a warning flare of the unrecognized pain that was consuming me.

The rest of the conference was agony. I moved my body like a hollow shell, forcing myself into sessions, smiling when I had to, all while wanting to scream until my lungs gave out. What would people think if I broke down in the convention center crying, raging in front of colleagues and strangers alike? Every word, every glance, every laugh felt like sandpaper on my nerves.

Meanwhile, my wife thrived in that environment. She was well-known, well-liked, constantly stopping to talk with people in the halls of the Caribe Royale Conference Center. I, on the other hand, could barely hold it together.

There was one moment I thought I would unravel completely. My wife was speaking with a man she had collaborated with over the past year. Their professional relationship had always unsettled me. Back in January, when I surprised her on a work trip, I found his backpack in her hotel room. I never forgot it. That unease simmered quietly in the background, feeding my insecurity. By June, those jealous thoughts had swollen into something poisonous, fueling the implosion I couldn't escape.

That moment in the hallway became a breaking point. My wife wanted to introduce me to this man she had worked with. As we approached, she lit up, touching his shoulder, smiling, eager to get his attention. She's naturally friendly, the kind of person whose warmth could easily be mistaken for flirting. But in my fractured state of mind, I was certain that's exactly what it was.

Jealousy hit me like a flood. I shrank inside myself, feeling small, cowering beneath the weight of my own thoughts. Rage coursed through me, hot and consuming, and I gripped tightly just to stay upright in that cold hallway. I knew something inside me was broken, but in that moment, all the blame landed squarely on my wife. Looking back, I see it wasn't her at all, it was my undiagnosed depression. At the time, though, I thought the storm had peaked. I had no idea how much worse it would get.

After that, tears became my unwelcome companions. They came more often than I had ever known, streaming down my face without warning. At night, when everyone was asleep, I would bury my head and let them flow, ashamed to be caught crying. The sadness was relentless, a heavy shadow pressing down on my chest, pulling me under.

The worst part was not knowing why. The tears poured out of me like a river, but the reasons stayed hidden, shrouded in darkness. I was drowning in a sea of sorrow, clawing for a lifeline, unable to make sense of the storm raging inside me.

No one around me understood what was happening. Friends and family, oblivious to the battle raging inside me, tried to make sense of the invisible chains that held me captive. All I saw in their eyes was judgment. The truth, however, escaped us all. I was trapped in a web of emotions I couldn't untangle, a maze of thoughts I couldn't escape. Each day, anger consumed me. Angry toward everyone and everything. It bulldozed through my marriage, ripping it apart piece by piece. My wife blamed me, unaware that something deeper was raging within. To her, it was simple: I was the problem. And in some ways, she was right, because all I could say was that I was angry at her.

But telling your wife you're angry at her does nothing to heal a marriage. It only deepens the divide. What I didn't understand then was how depression in men often disguises itself as anger, irritation, or withdrawal. Yet, instead of being recognized for what it is, it gets dismissed as character flaws.

For men, depression lives in the shadows of stigma. Society tells us to be strong, unshakable, and resilient. To show emotion is to risk being seen as weak. Masculinity itself has been redefined into something rigid and unforgiving, where anger, jealousy, and resentment are treated as evidence of failure rather than symptoms of pain. Few stop to ask what's beneath it. Few check on the man who is drowning in silence.

And so we suffer alone, often believing there is only one way out. By the time anyone notices, it can already be too late. Reaching for help feels impossible when the world sees you as the problem instead of the patient.

Never before had I experienced such a profound disconnection from the world around me. Life, once vibrant and full of purpose, faded into a monotonous gray haze. Days bled into one another until I was left questioning my very existence. The weight of this invisible burden grew heavier with each passing moment, pressing me toward a crossroads between life and death. I asked myself: If I choose life, will it mean forty more years of this joyless existence? Where do I turn? How do I go on?

My mind was so clouded by despair that I forgot the power of Jesus, the very one I had been raised to know. In turning away from Him, I had turned away from my only true source of help. Yet in His mercy, He reminded me of my faith. Amid the turmoil, I began to seek solace in the only place I knew could hold answers: the Bible.

When I finally turned to the Word, I found a glimmer of hope. Within its pages, I began a journey of rediscovery, searching for wisdom and understanding only God could provide. The stories of resilience, forgiveness, and faith shone like a guiding light through my darkness, reminding me that I was not alone.

Slowly, the biblical messages of compassion and love breathed a renewed sense of purpose into me, unveiling a path toward healing. Through faith, I began to untangle the depths of my pain and found strength in the timeless truths of Scripture.

It's easier for me to write about my faith now than it was to hold on to it then. In my lowest moments, I was stripped of joy and almost emptied of belief. It felt like climbing out of a pit, only to slide back down again. Satan clawing at me, pulling me into the darkness. Time after time, I tried to escape, only to fall. But even there, in that cycle of despair, God's Word never let go of me.

This book is a chronicle of the events that unfolded in the wake of that fateful day at the Caribe Royale Resort, a journey that has stretched over two years, carrying me out of darkness toward a glimmer of light at the end of the tunnel. It is a testament to the resilience of the human spirit and, more importantly, to the invincible strength that comes only from God.

As I walk this road of self-discovery, I invite you to walk with me, to bear witness to the transformative power of facing our inner battles, rediscovering faith, and experiencing the healing grace of Jesus.

Little did I know, when I first stepped through the doors of that hotel, that my life was about to change forever. The wave struck me, unyielding and relentless, and I was left to navigate the treacherous waters that followed.

This is my story. The story of the day depression crashed into me, and the journey that carried me toward hope.

CHAPTER 2

◇◇◇◇◇◇◇◇◇◇◇◇◇◇◇◇◇◇

Beneath the Sunshine:

Shadows of the Mind

When the darkness struck me that June day, confusion immediately consumed my mind like a dense fog, erasing any trace of clarity. What is wrong with me? That question echoed endlessly, bouncing through every corner of my thoughts. As the days passed, I sank deeper into a sea of self-doubt, searching desperately for answers yet finding no one I could turn to for help.

I had never felt anything like this before, mentally or emotionally. Yes, I had experienced sadness in my life, but this was something entirely different. In the past, joy may have slipped away for a moment, but it always returned, always felt within reach. This time was different. Every door I turned toward slammed shut, leaving me empty and hopeless. I knew something was terribly wrong. I was overwhelmed, angry, irritable, jealous, joyless. I had felt each of these emotions separately before, but together they created a suffocating storm that left me unable to think or function.

Depression wasn't even on my radar. The signs and symptoms cast a shadow over my existence, moving stealthily like a predator, ready to pounce on any glimmer of joy that dared to shine through. I yearned for happiness, but it slipped through my fingers like grains of sand. The answers I needed seemed just out of reach, like running up a wall only to slide back down again. No clarity, only confusion and emptiness.

Honestly, I thought I was either having a breakdown or facing a midlife crisis. Depression? That word never even crossed my mind. Why would I be depressed? Never in a million years did I imagine that I could be caught in its grip. I didn't know then how differently men can experience depression, or how complex the symptoms can be. Depression is like an intricate song of emotions, and while it plays its melody in both men and women, the tune is often different, each movement unique, yet equally heavy.

For men, depression often hides beneath a cloak of stoicism and withdrawal. It becomes a silent struggle, buried under the weight of societal expectations and the pressure to conform to rigid norms of masculinity. Masculinity is important, and I believe men are different from women, called to lead in ways that matter. Yet, the world's redefinition of masculinity has twisted those expectations, leaving many of us burdened and misunderstood.

As a result, the signs of depression in men may look different, making it harder to recognize what's truly happening. One of the most common symptoms is anger. While women may also experience anger, it often emerges more intensely in men as a response to depression. This anger can show up as irritability, sudden outbursts, or a constant simmering frustration that seeps into daily interactions. The turmoil brews within, spilling outward toward those closest, often without men fully understanding why.

Looking back now, it all makes sense. My days were filled with anger, most of it directed at my family, especially my wife. I lashed out over everything. Each outburst was followed by withdrawal, leaving a silence that only deepened the divide. My marriage began to suffer almost immediately. Irritability and frustration would boil over into another outburst, then retreat into withdrawal again. It was a cycle that repeated itself day after day, week after week.

My wife stood at the front line of my emotions during those first few months. Not knowing what was happening with me, she turned the blame back on me, which only fueled my pain further. The cycle became an awful loop, one that felt impossible to break.

One of my worst moments in the early stages of my breakdown happened on a humid evening near the beach, just over the bridge, in the parking lot of the Anna Maria Oyster House. Even now, as I write this, I can feel the raw emotions of that night. The memory cuts into me like a sharp knife. Strangely, I can't remember exactly what was said or what triggered the meltdown. I only know that something set me off, and the anger spewed from me like flames. The rage was intense. I was there with my wife, my daughter, and a close friend.

That day had been picture-perfect. We'd set up our little camp just a few feet from the Gulf, on the soft white sand of Holmes Beach at Anna Maria Island, AMI, as we Lakelanders call it. My wife and I played with our daughter for hours, digging in the sand and building castles. We raced into the waves and waded out until the warm water reached our chests. The sun blazed above us the entire day, making it feel like a scene from a dream vacation. But for me, it was a nightmare hiding in plain sight.

Later that evening, while waiting outside the restaurant for our table, my thoughts spiraled out of control. I was suddenly furious with my wife. We were reminiscing about a recent trip that hadn't gone well, and she mentioned that a colleague had recommended a restaurant we visited. But I was the one who had chosen that place. Such a small thing, so insignificant, yet it ignited me. That's where my mind was at the time: trapped in resentment.

I know what you're probably thinking: This guy is crazy. This guy is a narcissist. And honestly, I felt that way myself. The resentment burned so deeply that it didn't even make sense to me. Anger and bitterness fused together inside me like a toxic storm. Overwhelmed, I stormed away from my family and our friend, pacing to the far side of the parking lot, stewing in my turmoil. I kicked at the sand like a frustrated child, overcome with emotions I couldn't control. Eventually, though I don't remember why, I returned to my family, still angry, still lost, and more broken than I realized.

After rejoining the group, we sat down for dinner. But my mind wouldn't quiet. What do they think of me? Do they see me as weak now? Am I the kind of man women look down upon because of this breakdown? I ate in silence, my thoughts spiraling, and later drove the hour and a half home pretending nothing was wrong. That night blurred into fragments in my memory. I don't even recall what brought me back across the parking lot to my family. What I do remember is getting home, pouring a glass of whiskey, shutting off the lights, and crying myself to sleep, ashamed, broken, and alone. The embarrassment and sadness from that night still haunt me today.

For many men, depression takes the form of emotional numbness, an emptiness that strips the world of its color. Life, once vibrant, fades into dull shades of gray. That was me. The spark that had fueled my passions flickered and died, swallowed by the void of inner struggle. I felt detached from my own emotions, as if I were watching life happen from a distance. It was confusing, even terrifying screaming out for help, but only managing to scream at the people I loved most.

This emotional blunting pulled me further from my family. I couldn't connect the dots, couldn't understand the emptiness, only that I was drowning in it alone. Activities that once brought joy no longer mattered. Hobbies, relationships, even simple daily routines lost their meaning, leaving a hole I couldn't fill. Worst of all, my marriage, the most important relationship in my life, was unraveling.

I struggled to find any joy with my wife. The cycle of irritation and anger never stopped. I judged everything she did, and each small thing triggered me into another spiral. Jealousy consumed me. Every time she gave her attention to someone else, I fell deeper into resentment. It was a toxic loop, dragging me toward rock bottom. I clawed desperately for a way out, but every time I reached up, no hand was there to grab. I was utterly, devastatingly alone.

One of the greatest challenges men face in recognizing their depression lies in the society that surrounds them. From a young age, we are told to be strong, resilient, and self-reliant. Those expectations, however, become walls, intimidating barriers that keep us from seeking help or even admitting to ourselves that we're struggling. Vulnerability is too often equated with weakness, a direct contradiction to the world's definition of masculinity that we've been conditioned to uphold.

This stigma, combined with a limited understanding of mental health, leaves men isolated and confused. The cultural narrative whispers that depression is weakness, convincing us to fight our demons in silence. For me, that script played out perfectly. I wasn't sure what was happening inside me, only that I was supposed to be "the strong one." But I couldn't be. I didn't even have the strength to go on. I told myself over and over: You're weak. Buck up. Be a man. Meanwhile, depression pinned me down, tightening its grip on every part of my life.

I wanted so badly to reach out, to share what was happening within me. But instead, I retreated into myself, internalizing the anguish until it consumed me. When I look back at photos from that time, I see a sad and joyless man, forcing smiles to mask the storm inside.

I still believe masculinity matters, but real strength is not about burying your emotions. Real strength means facing them. It means having the courage to talk with someone you trust. As men, we have to support each other and change the cultural script around depression. We have to change the way we talk to ourselves, recognize the symptoms for what they are, and be willing to open up to the women and men in our lives.

Breaking these barriers is the only way forward. Only then can we begin to dismantle the stigma that chains men in silence and finally learn how to stand together against depression.

The journey toward understanding and acceptance is rarely straightforward. For men, navigating the twisting path of depression means wrestling with despair while carrying the weight of society's expectations. Breaking through stigma and confronting the silence around men's mental health is no easy task. Yet it is necessary because only by unraveling these complexities can men find solace, seek help, and step into a healing journey that leads to self-discovery and emotional well-being.

In the early months of my depression, I had no idea how to process what I was feeling. I didn't even recognize it as depression, let alone find the words to explain it to my wife. To her, I was simply lashing out. She saw me as the one with the problem and in truth, I was, but not in the way either of us understood. The walls built by stigma stood tall between us. For years, I couldn't break them down. My only relief came through tears, alcohol, and eventually, a slow return to my faith.

My descent to rock bottom was sudden and violent. One moment, I felt like I was at the top of the roller coaster; the next, I was plummeting without warning, unbuckled, unsure of how, or if, I would land. I call it the summer of "what's wrong with me." June and July of 2021 were the darkest months of my life, marking the beginning of the hardest years I have ever endured.

That summer unfolded like a relentless storm, testing the limits of my emotional strength. On the day depression first crashed over me, I should have felt joy. I was surrounded by my wife, my daughter, and friends at a party. But joy was out of reach. Instead, the weight of despair pressed down on me. The mask of happiness grew heavier by the hour, and I found myself triggered into irritation and rage at every turn.

At one point, the group wanted to take a photo together. The last thing I wanted was to capture that moment, but I forced myself into the photo booth. That picture still lives on my phone. When I look at it now, I see the truth: a man silently screaming in a crowded room. I don't think anyone noticed. That's the reality of depression in men: you can feel utterly alone even when surrounded by people.

I wish I had known what was happening that night. It might have spared me, and my family, so much loneliness and heartache. That's why I speak out now. Men must learn to recognize the early symptoms of depression, and those around them must learn how to respond with understanding and support. Without that support, the spiral often ends badly. And no man, or his family, should have to endure that in silence.

We already feel isolated in our depression, and being seen as a burden only deepens that loneliness. For me, the 1920s party was just the beginning of my unraveling. Things were about to get worse before they ever got better.

That summer carried us to the serene shores of Pensacola Beach, Florida. But even the gentle rhythm of the waves couldn't calm the storm inside me. My emotions, like a violent supercell, battered against the cracks in my mind. Anger became my constant companion, unwelcome, corrosive, and relentless. It poisoned every experience, leaving nothing untouched.

My wife, usually my anchor, now looked at me with worry and fear. I could see it in her eyes, and instead of pulling me closer to her, it fueled my frustration. I tried to apologize, to patch the widening rift, to fix the damage I was causing. But because I didn't yet realize I was battling depression, all of my efforts were hollow. Nothing worked.

She was in Pensacola for work, and my daughter, our five-pound Maltese puppy, and I joined her. Each day, she traveled to Milton, Florida, for her assignment, and I drove her there. That drive became a battlefield for my thoughts. My emotions raged the entire way, circling around jealousy and suspicion. I obsessed over the people she would see there, and especially over the man she had been emailing during what was supposed to have been our family trip earlier that summer. The anger consumed me, and I couldn't stop feeding it.

I could not fight the jealousy and anger that coursed through my veins. Every morning, my daughter, my little Maltese, and I would drop my wife off at the high school in Milton, and then I would break down, sobbing on the drive back to Pensacola. (I'll share more about those tears in a later chapter.)

As a believer in Christ, I knew I needed God. I just didn't know how to get past the emotions strangling me so I could truly lean on Him. During those drives, I blasted Elevation Worship's "Rattle" and Maverick City's "Thank You God" on repeat, hoping for some scrap of solace and understanding. Looking back now, I think those songs were the first small spark that pulled me toward my faith again, reminding me, however faintly, that God is in control.

At the time, though, I had no faith I would be okay. No clue what was happening. No idea things could still get worse. Even today, when I hear those songs, I'm transported back to those drives: the sobs, the despair, and the sense that healing was nowhere in sight.

One dinner at a beachfront restaurant in Pensacola epitomized the depth of my spiral. The anger simmering inside me finally boiled over, burning away any logic or restraint. That evening should have been beautiful. We were seated at a waterfront seafood restaurant, the room glowing with soft light. A glass tank brimmed with tropical fish, and through the nearby window came the muffled rhythm of the bay's waves.

But none of it mattered. I walked into that place already lit with rage, ready for a fight. My mind was spinning out of control, frustration and anger spilling over everything. Against my better judgment, I ordered a glass of red wine as soon as I sat down, something that felt alien to me, especially in front of my daughter. I never drank in public, let alone with her watching. Yet there it was: a 2018 Cambria Pinot Noir, sitting on the table between us.

It was as if my very essence had been distorted, poisoned by the darkness I couldn't understand. Looking back, that glass of wine marked the beginning of a dangerous belief: that alcohol could somehow save me.

Get a buzz and forget about life, that was the only thought running through my mind. My wife and I barely survived that dinner. I don't remember eating. The tension was so thick I'm certain even the server felt it every time she came by the table. I was relieved when it ended, but relief was hollow; there was nowhere to escape except driving my family back to the hotel.

The car ride was silent, heavy, and suffocating. We didn't speak. I sat behind the wheel, still unraveling. The drive from the beach across Pensacola Bay seemed endless. Once we reached the room, the weight inside me only grew. I honestly thought about sleeping in the car, convinced I couldn't bear being in the same room with them.

Even in their presence, I was utterly alone. This wasn't the solitude of an introvert, it was a crushing loneliness that made me question whether I even wanted to exist. The hurt inside me was raw, untraceable, and impossible to explain. Those memories are seared into my soul. And the summer had only just begun.

Next came Indiana, another stop in what I call the summer of despair. My emotions spiraled further out of control. Normally, returning to my small hometown filled me with peace: the scent of freshly cut hay, the green rows of corn stretching along the paved country roads, the easy rhythm of summer in the country. But this time was different. This time, I was living a nightmare.

Around my parents, I felt a crushing obligation to hide everything. I couldn't let them see how broken I was. "Don't show weakness. Be a man," I told myself. I carried that lie like armor. No matter what, I would not let them see my pain. Pretending to be okay was exhausting. The mask I wore grew heavier by the day, and the thought of them discovering my truth filled me with shame. In their eyes, I wanted to be strong, not fragile, not damaged.

One night, we went to the Beef House, a legendary restaurant near the Indiana–Illinois border. For me, it was a place steeped in memories: high school cross-country and track championship dinners, swim team celebrations, even my junior and senior proms in the banquet hall. I had grown up on their famously tender ribeye and those steaming hot yeast rolls with apple butter and strawberry jam.

But this time, the Beef House was different. My exhaustion was complete. I was ready for life to end. I ordered the ribeye out of habit, but I could barely touch it. When the broccoli and cheddar soup arrived, all I could feel was the deep emptiness gnawing at me.

I couldn't stomach it. I prayed my mom and dad wouldn't see through the mask I wore. I wanted it all to end, but instead, I forced myself to fake a smile, any smile.

As a man, I was raised to be strong, to lead without faltering. Admitting I was struggling felt like betraying everything I had been taught. I tried to protect my family from the weight of what I carried inside, thinking that if I hid it well enough, they could go on seeing me as the steady foundation they believed I was.

What I didn't realize was that the more I hid, the more I drifted into isolation. I pushed away the support I so badly needed. As I battled this silent war within myself, the loneliness deepened. The depression became heavier. There was no one I felt I could talk to, no one who I believed would truly understand if I did.

And still, the summer from hell wasn't over.

Another painful moment that summer was our wedding anniversary. As the date approached, my heart was torn between excitement and apprehension. It should have been a day of celebration, a chance to cherish the bond my wife and I shared. But instead, an overwhelming sadness and loneliness rooted itself deep inside me, fueled by the weight of my depression. I couldn't feel that bond, and I had no desire to celebrate.

My wife was buried in her work, consumed by relentless deadlines and responsibilities that devoured nearly every waking moment. I understood the importance of her career, especially during that summer, but the distance between us grew wider with each passing day.

When the evening of our anniversary arrived, I sat at the table with her, anger boiling inside me. She was still working, and I wanted to tell her how hurt I felt, how much I longed for her presence on this day, but my emotions had spiraled beyond control, knotted tight by depression. A battle raged within me, desperate to connect, yet unable to find the words.

In that moment, I realized her preoccupation with work wasn't the true problem. It was my depression that had driven a wedge between us, making it nearly impossible to express my needs clearly. I ached for her understanding and support, yet my struggles kept us from meeting on the same ground.

As we sat there, my heart heavy with unspoken words, I longed for the closeness we once shared. Our anniversary should have been filled with joy and love. Instead, it became a stark reminder of how much my depression had eroded our relationship. The darkness surrounding me wasn't just weighing me down, it was pulling her further and further away.

Was summer over yet?

As summer wore on, a weekend trip to North Carolina loomed, and with it came a sense of impending doom. I couldn't even make it to the destination before unraveling. The flight itself felt turbulent, a perfect reflection of the storm inside me. Emotions surged and crashed like relentless waves, leaving me gasping for air. Insecurity gnawed at me, sharp, unfamiliar, and unsettling.

What should have been a routine email exchange between my wife and a colleague quickly morphed into a tempest of jealousy and hurt. She was working under the pressure of a looming deadline, leading a project with a man who was emailing her his portion of the presentation. As we waited for our flight, from the gate at the St. Pete airport to takeoff, the two of them emailed back and forth nonstop. With every notification, my insecurity deepened, dragging me into a spiral I couldn't control.

I've always carried a thread of insecurity, but in that moment it became something darker. It consumed me, turning to extreme anger. I was furious with my wife. I couldn't understand why these emotions had me in such a chokehold, tearing at the very trust that had always bound us together. From the first moment at the gate to the time we landed back home, I wrestled with these awful, suffocating feelings.

I had been eager for this trip to the mountains of western Carolina to see my wife's parents, but the burden of my depression traveled with me like unwanted baggage. Despite my best efforts, anger and frustration shadowed me throughout the visit. I forced a cheerful facade, desperate not to burden my in-laws or spoil the family atmosphere, but the weight was too heavy.

The truth was, I simply wasn't able to face my depression then. Instead, it faced me, and in doing so, it robbed me of the chance to truly connect with the people I loved. Every moment was clouded by the shadow of sadness and anger I couldn't shake.

As the summer of "What's Wrong with Me?" unfolded, I found myself caught in a whirlwind of emotions, each one more bewildering than the last. The once steady landscape of my mind had become a maze of confusion, leaving me questioning who I was. It felt as if I had lost sight of myself, unable to make sense of the storm raging inside. I longed to be strong, but I didn't know what exactly needed fixing. I knew I was angry, yet I couldn't figure out how to quiet the fire.

My mind burned relentlessly. I felt as though I were on fire, desperate to leap out of my own body. I remember screaming aloud when no one was around, then forcing the cries back into silence whenever others drew near. Even the smallest decisions felt crushing, and I began pulling away from the people I loved, terrified they might see just how broken I was.

What I wanted most was paradoxical: I yearned for someone to ask if I was okay, to reach for me, yet I feared being asked at all. I wanted help but didn't know how to ask for it. I told myself that if the person I loved most didn't notice, then who ever would?

As days stretched into weeks, the weight only grew heavier. I searched endlessly within myself, analyzing every thought and emotion, hoping to uncover the source of my unraveling. But the deeper I went, the more lost I became. Clarity never came, only more darkness.

I longed for relief, for something steady to hold onto, but instead I discovered that facing my demons would require a strength I didn't think I possessed, a strength that could only come from God. The mask of happiness I wore for the world began to crack, exposing a raw and vulnerable self I had tried to keep hidden for years.

Realizing that I needed to face my depression head-on was terrifying but also strangely liberating. It marked the first step toward healing. As summer drew to its end, I didn't yet know that the road ahead would require even greater strength and surrender, leading me deeper into the labyrinth of my own emotions, and closer to the God who could bring me through it.

CHAPTER 3

The Unyielding Flood:

Tears Without End

For months after the onset of my depression, I was trapped in relentless emotional struggles, consumed by crying spells that seemed endless. Even in the middle of the day, a single thought about life could trigger waves of tears, leaving me drained and overwhelmed. The impact on daily life was devastating. Working from home became almost unbearable. I cried in silence, off camera, away from others, forcing myself to fake joy for colleagues who had no idea I was falling apart. My world felt upside down. Nearly every thought ended in sobbing, and I wept on and off, though mostly on, every day and night for weeks.

One incident from that time remains vivid, one of the most embarrassing breakdowns I've ever had. It happened one evening with my family when I completely unraveled. It began with me blurting out that I needed to leave and clear my head, a desperate urge to escape by driving away in despair.

I don't remember what triggered me that night, moments like that had become all too common, but I do remember the breakdown itself. I stormed into the garage, climbed into my wife's car, and sat behind the wheel with tears streaming down my face. I don't know why I thought driving made sense when I could barely see through the crying. I sat there sobbing, pounding the steering wheel, feeling like I simply couldn't take it anymore.

Even now, I can hear myself screaming in that garage: "I hate this, I hate this, I hate this." Writing about it makes the memory flood back as if it happened yesterday. My chest tightens as I type, and I can still feel the sting of tears pressing at the edges of my eyes.

I had faced many "rock bottoms" before, but this was a new one. To my shame, my wife and daughter followed me into the garage and witnessed everything,   me at my most vulnerable. Those early months of my breakdown were brutal, and I know my family often saw me at my worst. But this moment was different. It felt like a new low, one I couldn't hide.

I kept thinking, I'm a man. I have to be the strong one. Society had taught me not to cry, to tough it out, to keep it together for my wife and daughter. But it was too late. I was exposed, my pain laid bare in front of them. There I was, sitting in the car, pounding the steering wheel, screaming "I hate this!" The mask of strength had fallen. There was no more faking happiness. Joy simply didn't exist in my life anymore, and I couldn't pretend otherwise.

As the turmoil dragged on, I looked for relief in unhealthy ways, turning to whiskey for comfort and sleep. The old Ryan wasn't a drinker, not since college and the first years afterward, so this new habit felt foreign, even alarming. But it quickly grew into a problem. At night, I needed that buzz to quiet my emotions and numb the chaos inside.

Many nights ended the same way: crying myself to sleep, a glass of whiskey by my side. Alcohol became my refuge, a false friend that offered temporary peace. I longed for that moment when the lights went off, when I could sip until the rage, jealousy, and constant irritation finally dulled. I knew it wasn't real joy, but for a few hours my mind would stop racing. The whiskey calmed me enough to let exhaustion take over, and I would drift off, tears still wet on my face.

Men often turn to alcohol during depression for reasons rooted in culture as much as emotion. Society tells us to be stoic, to stay silent, to "man up" instead of reaching out. When feelings become unbearable, alcohol offers an easy escape, a way to numb the pain and silence the noise. That's exactly what I was doing: coping. Or at least trying to.

I had tried other ways to escape the fog when it first fell over me, but nothing worked. I wish I had turned to the Lord instead of the bottle. Looking back, I can see how tight the enemy's grip was on me, pulling me away from my faith and deeper into despair. I thought whiskey would ease my symptoms, and for a brief moment, it did. There was a rush of relief, even euphoria. But it was a lie. Alcohol is a depressant, and it only dragged me further into the pit.

The truth is, I trusted the bottom of a bottle more than I trusted my wife, a therapist, or even my God. Night after night, I looked forward to my drink. It became my crutch, my false friend, something I could cling to while hiding from the stigma of my emotions.

At the same time, I felt the crushing weight of expectations. I was supposed to be strong, unshakable. Instead, I found myself retreating into solitude. Many nights I left our bed to sleep on the couch in the living room, not because I wanted distance from my wife, but because I couldn't bear her seeing me break. I needed the cover of darkness, the silence of isolation, just to cry freely.

The stigma against men's vulnerability reinforced my shame. Each tear felt like failure. Each breakdown convinced me that I was less of a man. So I hid. I hid behind alcohol, behind solitude, behind silence. And in that hiding, the depression grew stronger.

 This pull toward isolation was shaped by deep-seated societal norms and ingrained gender expectations. For generations, men have been taught that vulnerability equals weakness, so we suppress emotions and bury struggles. At night, the darkness became my refuge. It gave me cover, a sense of security where I could break down unseen, confronting my turmoil away from the eyes of others.

The pressure to appear strong never let up. Being alone felt like the only way to escape the weight of pretending, especially in front of my wife and daughter. Solitude became a coping mechanism, not a healthy one, but the only space where I could wrestle with my emotions on my own terms. Yet looking back, I see how it also trapped me, keeping me from seeking the support I so badly needed.

During my lowest points, I had no desire to reach out. The idea of counseling felt impossible, and I'll explain later how badly those sessions failed. What I know now is that healing requires openness and honest communication, breaking the stigma, and leaning on the people who love us. Sometimes I wonder: if I had spoken up sooner, would I have healed faster?

The hardest part in those first two months was not even realizing what was happening to me. I wish I had tried to tell my wife, to let her in. Even though I didn't want her to see me like that, deep down I longed for her to notice, to ask, to pray with me. But every time I spoke to her, my words came out twisted, focused only on rage, anger, and jealousy. Instead of sharing my hurt, I blamed her for it. I told her how she made me angry, how she stirred my jealousy. Those conversations didn't bring us closer; they drove us down a dangerous road.

Whenever we did talk about it, it was always late at night, in bed, while I sobbed and my wife lay exhausted. Those conversations went nowhere. No resolution, no comfort, just more distance. After twelve years of marriage, we felt farther apart than ever.

I often wonder: if we had both understood depression in men, would things have been different? Would she have turned her judgment back to love? Would I have turned my anger into compassion, giving her, and myself, more grace?

As a man, I didn't know how to handle my sadness and anger. As a woman, my wife didn't know what to do with a husband who was both deeply sad and boiling with rage. I thought she was the cause of my feelings, and she thought I was an angry narcissist. The truth is, my anger scared her. She had never seen that side of me before. I would rage, then collapse into sobbing.

She never said it directly, but I'm certain she talked to her parents and friends about my outbursts. Most likely, she complained, and like so often happens, people took her side without searching for the deeper truth. That still stings, knowing my fury left her afraid in her own home and feeling she had to confide in others instead of me.

I should have been her rock, the one she leaned on, not the man who pushed her away. If I had been willing to face my emotions honestly with her, maybe I would have reached the word "depression" much sooner. Maybe we both would have been spared so much pain.

My journey through these emotional struggles serves as a stark reminder of the societal pressures placed on men and the urgent need to challenge these stereotypes. The belief that women think less of men when they cry is a deeply ingrained generalization that reinforces harmful gender norms. After living through this, I now believe that many women hold these assumptions, something that became painfully clear through my wife's responses.

That said, I still believe masculinity has an important role in our society. As a father, my daughter needs to see not only my strength and masculine side but also my emotional vulnerability. I have no desire to erase masculinity, blur gender distinctions, or remove the God-given differences between men and women. My faith, rooted in the Bible, affirms that there are two genders, each created with unique purposes. To me, the challenge is not to abandon masculinity, but to preserve it while breaking the stigma surrounding men's mental health.

The connection between men and suicide is alarming. Statistics consistently show that men are far more likely to die by suicide than women, even though women attempt it more often. This gap is often explained by the pressure on men to uphold traditional norms that discourage vulnerability and help-seeking. The stigma that labels emotional openness as weakness pushes many men into silence, worsening their struggles and increasing the risk of suicide.

I was one of those men, trying to make sense of my pain in the silence of my tears, wondering if I could keep going day after day. Suicide can feel like an easy way out. Since the onset of my depression and the writing of this book, I have lost two male family members to suicide, both of them suffering in silence.

It is essential to dismantle the barriers that prevent men from seeking help, promote mental health awareness, and create supportive environments where men feel safe to discuss their struggles without fear of judgment. Too often, vulnerability and emotional expression are misperceived as signs of weakness, traits wrongly associated with femininity. This mindset undermines men's emotional well-being and reinforces an unhealthy standard of masculinity that discourages openness and honesty.

True masculinity does not require silence. We can be strong and still express our feelings in healthy, appropriate ways. To foster real change, society must challenge these harmful beliefs and redefine masculinity to include emotional intelligence and vulnerability. When men are encouraged to express their emotions without ridicule, they can form deeper, more authentic connections with others, strengthening both relationships and overall well-being.

Faith plays an equally vital role in this process. Men should be encouraged to lean on God and the power of Jesus during seasons of struggle, trusting His strength rather than worldly definitions of manhood. Breaking free from the cultural expectations of what men "should" be, and embracing a more empathetic and faith-centered perspective, benefits not only men but also families and society as a whole.

Ultimately, it is essential to cultivate a compassionate environment where emotional expression is embraced, regardless of gender, and where vulnerability is understood as a true strength rather than a weakness.

CHAPTER 4

Rising from Weakness:

Finding Strength in His Word

In the depths of my depression, I finally turned back to my faith, seeking solace and hope amid the storm raging within me. I still believe the enemy had placed a cloak over my mind, and I allowed him to darken my thoughts, causing me to forget the power and love of Jesus. But when I realized what I was missing, His light broke through the darkness and began to shine upon my life.

One night, as I opened my Bible, my eyes fell upon a passage I had read countless times before, but never like this. Its words pierced my heart and soul, unveiling truths I had never truly grasped until that very moment. I believe it was the hand of God guiding me directly to these verses from 2 Corinthians 12:9–10 (ESV):

"But he said to me, 'My grace is sufficient for you, for my power is made perfect in weakness.' Therefore I will boast all the more gladly of my weaknesses, so that the power of Christ may rest upon me. For the sake of Christ, then, I am content with weaknesses, insults, hardships, persecutions, and calamities. For when I am weak, then I am strong."

As I read and reread these verses, their meaning began to settle deeper into my soul. I realized it was in my moments of vulnerability and helplessness that God's grace shone the brightest. During my depression, I had seen my weakness as a burden something shameful, something to hide and overcome as quickly as possible. My wife and daughter bore the weight of my struggles. I became a burden to them, and even to my wife's parents and friends, who stepped in to provide the comfort I could not. All the while, I was faking happiness everywhere I went, desperate for no one else to see how broken I was inside.

But Paul's words in this passage revealed a different perspective. He spoke of boasting in weakness, embracing it, because it was precisely in weakness that Christ's power was made known. For the first time, I began to see my fragility not as failure but as the very place where God wanted to meet me.

I never blamed God for my depression. I have always believed that God is good in all ways. This suffering was not from Him. It was the enemy clouding my mind in fog, pulling me further from sanity, and I didn't even realize it was happening. I wasn't resisting. I wasn't submitting fully to God, and in that gap the enemy seized his chance. Looking back, I see now that I let him get the best of me, but through this scripture I began to understand: God was my only way out. He was the only one who could save my life.

In Paul's words, I found a mirror of my own struggles. Like him, I cried out to God, begging for relief from the weight crushing my soul. I pleaded daily for Him to lift this burden. Some moments remain seared into my memory. One afternoon, I sat on our blue velvet couch in what we called the "blue room," sobbing uncontrollably, shouting at God for relief, feeling worse than blue. Over and over, I read 2 Corinthians 12:9–10, at least fifteen times in one sitting.

I remember crying out, "Please take this away from me! Please take this away from me!" My screams and wails echoed through the house, looping like a broken record. I was scraping the bottom of rock bottom, desperately searching for even the smallest glimmer of light. I was living in a darkness I didn't recognize, praying for sanctuary, praying for better days. Looking back, it is painful to remember, I had never been in such a place before: a place of suffocating darkness and unbearable loneliness.

This depression consumed me more than anything. I didn't recognize it at the time, or perhaps I refused to admit it, but I was teetering on the brink of no return. Life was filled with dread, and I often wondered how much longer I could hold on beneath the weight of such overwhelming emotions.

Drawing closer to God was the only thing that lessened the intensity of the darkness. I wish I could say that my depression vanished in a single miraculous moment while reading 2 Corinthians, but that is not my story. That was not God's timing. Still, it was through those verses that I began to grasp a profound truth. Each time I read them, a small seed of renewed faith took root within me, even though, in my darkest moments, I couldn't see or feel it. God was working for me in ways I did not yet understand.

Slowly, I started pulling out pieces of the text and connecting them to my own journey. I realized my weaknesses were not proof of failure but the very pathway drawing me closer to God. They forced me to rely on His strength instead of my own. And with that shift, I stopped trying to overcome my depression alone and instead began to invite Him to walk with me through the darkness.

Despite having been a Christian for as long as I can remember and growing up in the church, my struggle with depression caused me to lose sight of the very essence of my faith. I still cannot fully explain why I abandoned that faith the moment the fog of depression settled over me. Satan had a stronghold on my mind, an oppression that seemed to strip away my ability to see clearly. Part of his plan was to make me forget the very faith that could set me free.

I cried out to God, and I read His Word, but I did not place my trust in Him to help me. Our God is so good, and now I look back wondering what I was thinking. In that dark season, I struggled so much that I nearly gave up completely. The first thing I wish I had done was to put my faith in God, the God of healing, the God who rose from the grave.

I believe the enemy used my weaknesses to attack my mind. Satan is so evil that he will exploit any crack he finds. He is not omnipresent, he cannot be everywhere, but he has his army of fallen angels working to keep us down. I still don't fully understand what triggered my depression, but looking back, I can see that it had been creeping into my life for a long time. Now, as I move toward a healthier place, I wonder if my insecurities and past hurts opened the door for depression to take root.

Did the enemy use that small crack to enter my life? I cannot say with certainty, but I believe it came from a fracture in my faith. It wasn't until I began calling out to God while reading 2 Corinthians that I realized what was missing. I had let my weakness take control because I lacked true faith. That scripture became a gentle reminder, a lifeline thrown to me in my desperation. It was God's way of bringing me back, rekindling the flickering flame of belief in His faithfulness, and teaching me that His grace is sufficient for every need.

Yet even with this renewed understanding, I had to face the reality that overcoming depression was not an instant process. Though my faith was being rebuilt, I still carried the crushing weight of my emotions, a burden far too heavy to bear alone. Some days, hope felt unreachable, and the darkness threatened to consume me all over again.

It was as if I were trapped in a room without windows or doors, where every glimpse of an exit vanished as soon as I reached for it. In the midst of this relentless struggle, I turned again and again to 2 Corinthians, seeking peace and hope to break through the shadows that clouded my mind. Each time I read those verses, they became a stepping stone, an anchor for my unsteady faith, pushing me forward with a flicker of strength.

But the journey was far from smooth. For every two steps forward, despair seemed to yank me back, like a cruel undertow in the storm of my emotions. The darkness was persistent, revealing itself in the most unexpected moments, reminding me of its grip. I felt caught in a deafening tug-of-war between fragile hope and the temptation to let go completely.

The enemy worked tirelessly to overpower me. I was weak on

my own, allowing dark thoughts to burrow deep into my mind. Looking back now, I feel shame   shame for letting depression take hold, and shame for how I treated my wife during that season. I unpack that shame more deeply in a later chapter, but today I remind myself of God's grace. He does not measure my life by yesterday's mistakes. His grace is sufficient for me, and His power is made perfect in my weakness.

More than two years later, I often ask myself why I allowed my weakness to rule me when God had been there all along. Now I see the truth: just as Paul declared, I too can boast in my weakness so that the power of Christ may rest upon me.

In those moments of darkness, Paul's words reminded me that healing was not a single event but a process, one that required God's help and unfolded in His timing. It was never about a quick fix or an instant remedy, but about the gradual transformation of my heart and mind.

What once felt like weakness became stepping stones, drawing me into a deeper dependence on God and His sustaining power. Looking back, I now see that season as one of the darkest I have ever faced, yet also as a time of profound growth and spiritual rediscovery.

Through the truth of 2 Corinthians 12:9–10, I discovered comfort, hope, and the strength to endure. Finding that strength was not easy, and I know I could never have taken another step forward without God carrying me. His Word became a lifeline   anchoring me in faith and reminding me that even in my weakest moments, His strength was made perfect in me.

For when I am weak, then I am strong.

CHAPTER 5

◇◇◇◇◇◇◇◇◇◇◇◇◇◇◇◇◇◇◇◇

Fury Unleashed:

Confronting the Inner Storm

Anger, like a relentless hurricane, had crashed into my life and taken root in my heart and soul. No matter how hard I tried, I couldn't escape it. The shift was sudden: one moment I felt normal and happy, and the next it was as if someone had flipped a switch, turning my joy into rage. Each day brought a fresh wave of fury, a violent storm on the sea of frustration that threatened to pull me under.

This anger was unlike anything I had experienced before. Sure, I had been upset in the past, but this was different. This was consuming. It gripped me so tightly that I couldn't dig myself out or turn it off. It was a fire coursing through my veins, and when it reached my mind, I became someone I didn't recognize.

I don't think anger in men's depression gets talked about enough. It changes us. Looking back, I wonder why no one said anything to me. Maybe they noticed, but chose silence. Maybe it was easier to whisper behind my back than ask me what was wrong. Their judgment only added fuel to the fire. And I still ask myself, would I have healed faster if someone had simply asked me, Why are you so angry?

My journey through depression was marked by many difficult moments, but the anger I carried was perhaps the most bewildering of them all. It just wasn't like me to be angry all the time. The smallest things would set me off, and I couldn't control my temper. Once, I completely lost it because my wife answered a text while I was talking to her. How absurd is that? The anger was out of control. It became my constant companion, a toxic undercurrent that poisoned every corner of my life.

I had always prided myself on being calm and collected, the kind of person who rarely lost his temper. Yet here I was, consumed by a seething rage that was as unpredictable as it was overwhelming. I never knew what might trigger it, and it didn't matter where I was or who was around. My anger raged in public places, like the parking lot of the Oyster House in Anna Maria, and in the privacy of my bedroom late at night when I was trying to talk with my wife. Even when I was alone, I was still angry, and that's something I wouldn't wish on anyone. My reactions created a vicious cycle, dragging me from sadness to anger and back again.

What baffled me even more was the jealousy and resentment that anger stirred up. I resented those who seemed to live normal, happy lives, free from the torment that defined my own. I envied people who could experience joy without it being tainted by the dark cloud that hung over every moment for me.

Resentment was not new to me. Growing up, I often felt bitterness toward others, especially when I thought I had been wronged.

It was always wrapped in irritation, hostility, or even a desire for revenge. I would dwell on those feelings, replaying moments over and over again in my head. As I grew into adulthood, I learned how to manage those emotions and keep them from consuming me. But this time, resentment returned with reinforcements: rage, jealousy, and endless rumination.

And the person it landed on was my wife. I regret that deeply. She became the target of my darkest emotions, even when she had done nothing to deserve it. I wish I had carried that burden alone, but instead, I pulled her into the storm that was raging inside me.

And I didn't hold back on the emotions that came with it. For me, jealousy was one of the strongest and most destructive feelings that fueled the resentment, right alongside the anger. I was jealous of my wife and even of the people around her, and that jealousy fed my resentment toward her.

There are countless stories of the resentment, jealousy, and anger I unleashed on my wife, but one stands out vividly. My family and I were in Indiana visiting my parents, and I can still see it clearly in my mind. We were in a small grocery store in Covington, picking up a few items, nothing major. The nostalgia of that place should have brought me joy. I had been there countless times with my mom and grandma. But this visit was different.

My mom was checking out while my wife and I stood by the coolers, looking at the drinks. She lit up when she spotted a churro-flavored iced coffee and, with excitement, said that a man she had worked with on a project would love it because he loved churros. In that moment, my anger hit full force. Even now, I wonder why I reacted the way I did. It was such a small, silly thing. But at the time, I was in a full rage.

The resentment twisted into more jealousy, which only deepened the anger. I convinced myself my wife had wronged me, and I stormed away like a child. Looking back, I feel embarrassed by the way I acted in that little Midwestern grocery store. I was not behaving like the Christian I claimed to be, far from it.

If I had understood then that depression was fueling my anger, resentment, and jealousy, I hope I would have shown more kindness and been slower to anger. Even though the anger seeped into nearly every part of my life, it didn't show up at work. It was summer, a quieter season, and I think that helped. I faked my happiness there, stepping away from the computer when I needed to fall apart so no one would see my breakdowns on the virtual screen.

I did the same at church, with my parents, and as much as possible in public. I managed to hold it together well enough. But at home, my wife and child bore the brunt of my wrath. My anger never turned physical, but they lived on eggshells, never knowing when the next outburst would explode.

I could see the hurt in their eyes, the confusion as they tried to understand what had happened to the man they once knew. Raising my daughter was especially difficult. The smallest things she did infuriated me, and I was a terrible dad in those moments. The damage was done, and all I can do now is move forward, trying to be a better father in the present and future.

My marriage, once filled with love and laughter, had become strained, a battleground where anger was my weapon of choice. My rage scared my wife. At the time, I didn't realize she feared me. I never acted out physically, but my anger was explosive. Months later, I found a text she had sent to friends, hinting at how afraid she was of me. That discovery broke me. The last thing I ever wanted was for her to feel unsafe around me.

These outbursts weren't who I was. Why didn't she ask me what was wrong? Why did she confide in her friends instead of trying to help me? One of the hardest parts of all this was knowing she thought this anger defined me.

It was a vicious cycle. I would explode in anger, hurling hurtful words like daggers. Then, as the rage subsided, I was crushed by guilt and sadness. I would look at the aftermath and wonder how I had let things get this far. Anger became the clearest symptom of my depression, but it was also the one that pushed everyone away. The hard truth was, I didn't even know it was depression. If I had known that anger could be a symptom of depression in men, I might have gotten ahead of it. Could I have managed my emotions better if I had understood what was happening? Would I have leaned on God sooner?

The truth is, I could never have gotten through this without His power. All the anger and sadness churned inside me, but what I really needed was to cling to the one constant God. He was, and still is, the only one who can take away that anger.

Many nights I lay awake, tears streaming down my face, unable to comprehend what was happening to me. I didn't understand why I was so angry, why happiness seemed so far out of reach. I felt like I was losing control, trapped in a never-ending nightmare where anger ruled my life. At that time, I was living by the flesh, not by the Spirit. In my most vulnerable moments, I chose not to walk with Him, not to rest in His presence. I regret surrendering to my worldly mind and letting it dictate my emotions.

If I could go back, I wouldn't want to relive those nights of rage and regret. I was angry, restless, and far from walking like Jesus. My life was without peace, filled only with rage. Romans 8:6 says, "For to set the mind on the flesh is death, but to set the mind on the Spirit is life and peace" (ESV). My flesh was hostile to God, and the only way to find peace was to set my mind on the Spirit. Unfortunately, that shift took longer than I ever wanted. For two long, rage-filled years, the anger ravaged my life.

The worst part was that the anger didn't seem to have a clear cause. There were only a few real triggers, but no obvious reasons for the explosive outbursts. Most of it came from delusions born out of my insecurities in my relationship. I'll have to dive deeper into the subject of delusion in a later book, but at that time, I was internalizing everything and lashing out, especially at my wife. She never knew when I might lose it. When would my anger strike? It was like a beast lurking in the shadows, waiting to pounce at any moment.

I searched desperately for answers, but they remained just out of reach. I looked to the world for solutions, but there was no deliverance to be found there. The only way out was by the grace of God. Meanwhile, I wrestled with how to express and control this new, uncontrollable anger.

One moment stands out clearly. My wife and I were talking about where to eat while she was around some of her colleagues. One of them mentioned a place, and she lit up with excitement, an excitement I hadn't seen directed toward me in a long time. In my delusional thinking, I twisted her joy into an offense against me. Fueled by that distortion, I became enraged. I can still remember the blood surging through my veins, boiling hot with fury. Of course, I didn't handle it well, and it quickly spiraled into yet another argument.

Looking back, I see how the devil was ripping my life apart, stealing my joy and tearing at my marriage. I am deeply embarrassed by those moments. I regret so many of the things I said and did out of anger, especially toward my wife and daughter.

Sometimes I thought the anger might finally subside, or at least I hoped it would stop. And if, by some miracle, the anger did fade, it was quickly replaced by a deep, suffocating sadness. My joy was swallowed up by anger and sorrow. I'd felt sadness before, but never anything this heavy, this tangled with rage. It was the complete absence of joy. I begged for happiness to return and for the anger to leave, but I couldn't grasp either.

One moment stands out when I saw a picture of myself from that season of life. My wife and I were at an ax-throwing venue, a place buzzing with laughter and chatter. It was a desperate date night. Our marriage was in a bad place, and I had begged her to go out with me. I remember the night being fun, and for a few hours we enjoyed each other's company. But when I later saw the photo, I was shocked.

I looked rough, a ragged face, dark bags under my eyes, skin pale and sickly. I didn't look healthy at all. It was as if the anger had drained the life right out of me. I imagine I looked exactly like a man weighed down by depression. Yet at the time, I thought I was hiding it well. Looking back, I wonder how no one noticed, or why no one asked if I was okay. I looked like a man who had lost all joy, but no one close to me said a word. If I wasn't hiding it, what were people really thinking when they saw me?

Anger in men is often misunderstood. Too often, it gets mislabeled as narcissism or simply being a jerk. People are quick to judge angry men. I recently read an article advising women to avoid so-called narcissistic men, saying such men are just children who don't truly love, and that women will never find love with them. But what if there's more beneath the surface? What if the anger is a symptom of something deeper, like depression? Society needs to pause before judging and instead check on men who are acting out. Sometimes, waiting too long to notice means it's too late.

If not for God, I honestly don't know what would have happened to me. My depression pushed me to the edge. I hated life, and there were moments I didn't want to go on feeling the way I did. The anger was unbearable, and the sadness that followed was crushing. Only God knows how close I came to ending it all. But by His grace, that was not my outcome.

I felt isolated, as if I were fighting this battle alone, with no one beside me. It was like the universe itself was conspiring to keep me from peace. I was trapped between the relentless tide of anger and the abyss of despair.

As I reflect on the long haul of depression, my mind goes to Ephesians 6:10–18. In his letter to the Ephesians, Paul tells us to be strong in the Lord and in the strength of His might. He urges us to put on the whole armor of God, so that we can stand against the schemes of the devil. Depression is one of those schemes. Do not forget that: it is of the devil! And we cannot fight it on our own. I know because I tried and failed.

Paul reminds us that our battle is not against flesh and blood but against rulers, authorities, cosmic powers over darkness, and spiritual forces of evil. We have authority in Christ, but we must exercise it. At the time, I didn't have the strength to fight. I needed help. I needed Him. The devil wanted me dead. He wanted me to destroy myself. I had to take authority over the enemy. Because the truth is, we will all face battles, and some of them will come straight from the pits of hell, like depression. And the only way through is to keep standing, keep praying, and hold tightly to faith.

My mind was so bound by anger that I couldn't think clearly. Satan had me right where he wanted me, drowning in doubts. I doubted my worth, my purpose, whether anyone truly cared what happened to me. Instead of facing those doubts, I replaced them with anger. And when the anger faded, sadness swallowed me whole. At night, when I was most vulnerable, the enemy attacked with relentless thoughts, racing through my mind in the dark.

One night stands out. It was after 1 a.m. My anger had given way to crushing sadness. I was lying next to my wife, yet I felt completely alone. I had poured a few glasses of whiskey, hoping it would take the edge off. Instead, it only opened the floodgates. I started replaying every flaw, every failure, until I broke down sobbing. There I was, in bed with my wife, unable to share what I felt, crying uncontrollably beside her.

That night, I wished it would all just end. I couldn't believe how far I had fallen. Was I really thinking about suicide? Was I truly ready to end it all? Those weren't my thoughts, those were seeds planted by the enemy. Still, they tormented me. Like many nights before and after, I eventually cried myself to sleep, my pillow soaked, my face streaked with tears. Sleep was the only escape I had.

I've learned that in the pitch-black of the night, we must put on the full armor of God. It is the only way to stand against the enemy, against the spiritual forces of evil. As Paul urged the Ephesians, we must remain alert and persevere. For me, persevering through the grace of God was the only reason I kept going, the only reason I didn't end it all.

In the depths of despair, I often questioned whether I could survive another day. The anger had become a prison, locking me away from the world and from the people I loved most. Yet somewhere deep inside, by God's mercy, a faint glimmer of hope began to shine through the darkness. That spark told me I had to keep turning to the Word, keep fighting to understand, and keep pressing to overcome the anger that threatened to consume me. Only then could I find my way back into the light.

—◦◊◦—

CHAPTER 6

Fear Not,

Stand Firm

In the pit of hopelessness, when the weight of the world felt too heavy to bear, one scripture became my lifeline, a beacon of hope piercing the darkness. After the first waves of depression hit, I managed to gather my thoughts, if only for a moment, and remember what I truly believed: the power of God. I found myself drawn to the miraculous story of Moses and the Israelites, trapped in the wilderness with their backs against the sea. That passage became deeply personal to me. Exodus 14:13-14 whispered to my soul, urging me to "fear not, stand firm." Those words, simple yet profound, became the anchor of my journey toward understanding that God was always in control.

"Fear not, stand firm, and see the salvation of the Lord, which he will work for you today. For the Egyptians whom you see today, you shall never see again. The Lord will fight for you, and you have only to be silent."   Exodus 14:13-14

At that pivotal moment in my life, I was teetering on the edge of losing my faith completely. Honestly, I felt on the verge of losing everything. My life seemed worthless and unbearably sad, yet God was not finished with me. He had plans for my life to continue, and He gently guided me toward this scripture.

It was a Wednesday afternoon, strangely sunny. In Florida, the days were almost always bright, but to me, the light was muted. A gray filter seemed to cover my eyes, making every day feel cloudy and heavy. I hadn't truly seen the sun in my spirit for a long time. I was sitting on the blue velvet couch in the blue room, a place I often escaped to when I wanted to hide from everything, except my own mind. I had been fighting this darkness for some time and desperately needed to disconnect from reality. Though it was a workday, I couldn't keep pretending to be fine. I needed a break.

I work from home, so I slipped away to that blue room, hoping for peace. The irony was hard to ignore. The room was bright, flooded with light from a large picture window and sliding doors. Yet, inside, I couldn't feel any of that brightness.

As I sat on that couch, the tears came, uncontrollable and familiar by now. Sobbing, I scrolled aimlessly through my phone, desperate to distract my mind. If it hadn't been a workday, I probably would have reached for whiskey, but instead, I turned to social media and shopping apps.

During that season, shopping had become a habit. I kept buying things I didn't need, chasing tiny sparks of happiness that never lasted. A few years later, my wife would tell me she always knew I was unraveling when packages began showing up at our doorstep, four, sometimes five at a time. After a few minutes of searching for something to buy, hoping to capture even a fleeting moment of joy…

I couldn't find anything I wanted, and that was becoming the story of my life. Nothing seemed capable of making me happy. At that moment, the Holy Spirit nudged me toward the Bible app, the one I should have opened first. I tapped it open and sat there in silence. When you first launch the app, the verse of the day appears at the top of the screen. I remember staring at it, though I can't recall the exact verse or even if I read it clearly. My eyes were blurred with tears. Still, deep down, I knew my only way out of this darkness was through the power of Jesus. Yet, for reasons I couldn't fully grasp, I couldn't hold on to that truth enough to climb out of the pit of depression.

Even in prayer, I felt stuck, like I was knee-deep in mud, struggling to praise my way out. But then, I finally landed on the verse I needed. Exodus 14 became my catalyst, a scripture I clung to daily. The darkness of depression had clouded my vision, and I felt as though I was trapped in the wilderness, hemmed in by an unforgiving sea of gloom. The painful truth was that I was acting just like the Israelites: impatient, fearful, and unwilling to trust, waiting for a rescue. I wrestled with God's plan and questioned His protection. Even though I had witnessed miracles in my own life, I still struggled to trust Him to save me this time.

I wish I could say I was more like Moses: faithful, courageous, and obedient, pointing my eyes toward God. His trust in the Lord enabled him to lead the Israelites out of bondage, and his bravery helped them endure the hardest moments. But when my battle began, I didn't have that kind of faith. I didn't have courage at all. What I carried instead was the opposite: fear and unbelief.

My season of depression felt like the moment Pharaoh's army

drew near to the people of Israel. I looked at my depression as if it were the Egyptians themselves marching steadily toward me, threatening to overtake me. The weight of it grew larger than life, closing in like chariots and soldiers advancing without mercy. Fear consumed me, and I questioned whether I could endure the emotions and negative thoughts pressing down on me. Was I destined to die in the wilderness of my mind? Was death the only way out of depression? I even wondered if it would be better to live a life trapped in depression than to die with it.

But just as the Israelites' story did not end there, neither did mine. The parallel between my struggle and their journey in Exodus 14 became clearer each day. I felt the suffocating waters of despair surrounding me, just as they felt the Egyptian army pressing hard against them. Yet, like them, my story wasn't over. I fought to push death away, and in desperation, I began to pray and believe that the Lord could perform a miraculous intervention.

Just as He had driven back the sea to make a way for His people, I prayed fervently that He would split the sea of my troubles so I could walk toward healing and hope. That's when Moses' words pierced my heart. I collapsed to the floor in a fetal position, tears streaming down my face, reading the passage over and over: "The Lord will fight for you, and you have only to be silent."

Silence? What did that mean for me? Stay quiet? Stay still? It felt like the opposite of what I was doing, crying out, begging God to take the depression from me. But slowly, I began to understand. The verse wasn't telling me to suppress my cries; it was calling me to surrender my fight and let God take over.

So I sat in the stillness of our blue room, meditating on Exodus 14:14, holding tightly to the promise that He would fight for me.

In those moments, I realized I didn't have to carry the weight of my struggles alone. The same God who fought for the Israelites was willing to fight for me too. All I had to do was trust Him and rest in His presence.

Just as the Lord told Moses to instruct the people of Israel to go forward, I felt the call to move forward in my own life, to rest in the silence of the Lord. Depression is not from God, and through Him, we have the power to overcome it. Sometimes, we need to be the ones who remind others of His promises and His healing power.

I often wish someone had been in my corner early on in my depression to remind me of God's strength. But I had no one. Perhaps I should have shared my struggle more openly, and maybe people would have come alongside me. Instead, I wasn't honest about my feelings with anyone. On the outside, I looked like a man consumed by anger, yelling, pouting, fuming all the time. That's typically the kind of man people shun, blame, or gossip about. Many assume such behavior is narcissism, but sometimes there's something deeper going on, something that requires compassion and support from loved ones.

I understand that I was at fault for the way I treated the people I love, and I'll go into more detail about the blame and shame I carry in a later chapter. Still, I also know this: if I ever encounter someone walking through a similar struggle, I will remind them to lift their staff, stretch it out over their depression, and trust God to split that sea so they can walk across on dry ground.

In my own journey, it took more than a year before my loved ones began to understand what was wrong with me. Even now, I'm not sure they fully grasp it, but I know they are relieved to see a changed man, even though their support didn't play much part in that transformation. During those dark times, I wanted to burst out of my skin and tell people what was wrong with me. My wife was the first to begin to understand, though that didn't make our relationship any easier. Like most people, she wasn't educated about depression in men. What it looks like, what it does, and how to respond. Honestly, I didn't realize it was depression at first either.

I don't blame her for not knowing or understanding. But now, I want to turn that ignorance into advocacy, to help other men going through what I endured, and to help their loved ones learn how to support them before it's too late.

I know that God has split my sea and shown me dry land. It took me a few years to cross it, but I did. When I first began writing this book, I was still in the process of healing. Now, as I write this chapter, I can say with gratitude that I feel better mentally, and the progress has been remarkable, thank the Lord.

Depression is something God can heal in an instant for some, never to return. But I also believe healing can come slowly, over time. Mine did. We are on God's timeline, not our own. He is in control of it all. That's why Moses' words in Exodus ring so true: "Fear not, stand firm."

During the darkest times of my depression, I feared my own end. Would I become suicidal and choose to take my life? I often told myself I couldn't go on like this, though I never fully admitted to myself what I meant by those words. I feared I wouldn't make it.

Even now, fear is something I battle daily in connection to depression. It dominated my life for two years, and sometimes I still wonder if it will return. It hit me suddenly and violently the first time. Could it strike again in the blink of an eye? Whenever I get irritated or unsettled, I pause and ask myself, Is it coming back?

Even while walking across dry land, I wondered if the waters would suddenly collapse, flooding over me, pushing me down, filling my lungs, leaving me gasping for air, drowning alone where no one would even know. I have feared that would be the end of me.

But then I remember the words: "Fear not, stand firm." Fear paralyzes us. It distracts us from faith. And fear is not from God. As Paul reminds us in 2 Timothy 1:7, "For God gave us a spirit not of fear but of power and love and self-control."

We must cling to that truth. God is always in control, and we need to let that truth sink deep into our souls.

God commands our steps. Just as He told Moses in Exodus 14, "Tell the people of Israel to turn back and encamp...facing it, by the sea," so too does He give us direction. We must be prepared, strong in our faith, and always remember that God will guide us. Our steps are planned, and our part is to trust Him.

I was not prepared when depression struck. It exposed a deep spiritual darkness in me. The weight of it was so heavy that I couldn't hear God's voice. Satan is a powerful force if we allow him to be, but we must resist and turn our minds back to the Lord.

In Exodus 14, when the Egyptians saw the Lord in the pillar of fire and cloud, they panicked and fled. Satan reacts the same way in our battles. He flees at the power of the Lord. We must take hold of that power and apply it to our depression.

The Lord gave Moses authority to push the waters back over the Egyptians, drowning them. He gives us that same authority. Through Him, we are equipped to push back the waters of depression until they drown. By God's power, we can step ahead of our depression and walk on dry ground toward healthy, restored thoughts.

The Lord saved Israel that day, leaving the Egyptians dead on the seashore. In the same way, He can save us from depression. I know how misunderstood depression can be. The Israelites walked with towering walls of water on either side, unsure if those waters would collapse. That's what depression feels like, the constant fear of being swallowed whole.

Life continues even as I write this. I'm living day by day through my healing. Recently, one evening, my family and I sat outside on the pool deck for dinner. It was a beautiful Florida night. The sun was setting, the pool water rippling gently, and a breeze rustled through the palm trees. Chili was on the menu, its aroma filling the air. I sat there with my wife and daughter, enjoying myself, something I hadn't felt for two long years.

Then, suddenly, something shifted in my mind. My wife said something small, yet it sparked a flash of jealousy, rage, and resentment. In that instant, I froze. Was this a relapse? Was I about to break down again? The fear was real, but I fought to push it aside.

God is stronger than fear. I was able to refocus, release the fear, and return to enjoying dinner with my family. That night reminded me of this truth: when I put Him first, I can trust that He is my rescuer, no matter the circumstances surrounding me.

Exodus 14 is a pivotal chapter, capturing a defining moment in

Israel's escape from slavery in Egypt. After being released, the Israelites were led out by Moses. But Pharaoh's heart hardened, and he pursued them. Trapped between the Red Sea and Pharaoh's army, the people were terrified. Moses encouraged them, then received power from God to part the sea. The Israelites walked through on dry land, and the Egyptian army was drowned.

God placed this passage in my life at the exact moment I needed saving. How many times have we read about Moses parting the waters? I've heard this story since childhood, sitting in the basement of my small Christian church during Sunday School. I've heard it sung in worship songs and preached from the pulpit countless times. I've even sung the line: "You split the sea so I could walk right through it, my fears are drowned in perfect love." But only now do I truly understand it.

For the first time in my life, God drew me directly to this verse. He put it in my heart, and as I read Exodus 14 on the Bible app, tears streamed down my face. I could barely see the screen, but the message was clear: my escape from depression was possible.

For the first time in my darkness, I believed God could free me from the chains that bound me to the prison wall. From that moment, my thinking began to shift. I started searching for purpose instead of surrendering to despair.

Exodus 14 became my pivot point. Those verses spoke to me of courage, trust, and reliance on the God who parts seas and delivers His people from the most desperate circumstances. My healing was not instant; it was slow and arduous, much like Israel's long journey through the wilderness. But I clung to Exodus 14:14 with determination: "The Lord will fight for you; you need only to be still."

I believed that, just as God parted the Red Sea, He could also make a way through my own impossible obstacles. His faithfulness and power were clear in scripture, and I knew they applied to my life as well. Like the Israelites, I needed courage to stand firm and trust His plan, and that trust became the anchor of my healing.

My turnaround had begun, but I knew it would take great courage and unwavering faith in God to navigate the turbulent waters of depression. As I continued to meditate on Exodus 14:13–14, I found comfort in the unshakable truth that God was in control. With each passing day, I began to realize that the Lord was fighting for me, even when I could not perceive it. And just as the Israelites emerged safely from the parted sea, I too began to glimpse the promise of a brighter tomorrow, a tomorrow free from the chains of depression and despair.

CHAPTER 7

◇◇◇◇◇◇◇◇◇◇◇◇◇◇◇◇◇◇

Awakening to the Truth:
Understanding My Depression

In the realm of male mental health, there lies a subtle yet profound truth: depression often wears a mask, disguising itself as something else entirely. This chapter explores my journey of discovering my depression and peeling back the layers that hid the darkness within me. At first, I had no idea that what I was battling was depression, because it appeared in ways I didn't recognize. Depression is a serious and complex condition that can deeply affect a person's life, even when they don't realize they are experiencing it.

I had no clue what was happening, which only made things worse. I knew something was terribly wrong, and I felt like I was losing my mind, but I never considered that it could be depression. When someone doesn't realize they're depressed, the challenge becomes even greater, because they may not seek the help and support they desperately need. Even though I sensed something was wrong, I didn't think I needed help for depression.

To those around me, my most visible symptom was anger. That led me to believe I needed anger management, when in truth I needed something far more urgent. Each day, I grew mentally worse, and in hindsight I can clearly see how close I was to self-destruction.

Because symptoms of depression in men often hide beneath other behaviors and emotions, it is crucial to recognize the hidden signs, seek help, and raise awareness about mental health. If you suspect that you or someone you love may be experiencing depression, reach out to a mental health professional for an accurate diagnosis and appropriate treatment.

While I fully believe that God can heal us completely, I also know that sometimes He works through people here on Earth. Depression is treatable, and early intervention can make all the difference in restoring a person's well-being and quality of life.

As I look back on those bewildering months of unraveling my mental breakdown, I feel compelled to share the personal stories and insights that surfaced both during and before that time. It was a season of profound transformation, though I had no idea of the true nature of the beast lurking within me. In searching my past, I've often asked myself: Was I always depressed? Had I always struggled to find joy? Had I always hated life?

Depression has a peculiar way of camouflaging itself, even when it is right in front of you. As a child, I was often withdrawn, preferring solitary activities over the company of others. That wasn't unusual in itself, yet I now wonder if it was an early sign of depression before I even knew what it was. My tendency to overthink, my fragile self-esteem, and the occasional waves of overwhelming sadness had long been part of the backdrop of my life.

In elementary school, I struggled to fit in with the other boys and often felt more accepted by girls. Even back in preschool, making friends never came easily. Recently, my mom converted our old VHS tapes to DVDs, and I watched a Halloween parade video from those early years. I was dressed in a flowy purple clown costume complete with the dreaded red sponge nose. Ironically, I've always hated clowns, so I'm still not sure how that costume came to be. In the video, I wasn't smiling. In fact, I had a full-on frown, walking in the parade like I'd rather be anywhere else. The other children were waving, laughing, and enjoying themselves, while I looked utterly disengaged. Was it simply because I hated clowns, or was it an early sign of social anxiety, or even childhood depression?

I wonder if my parents noticed. Did they simply think I was different? Was this one of the first hints of how society dismisses boys who show signs of depression?

Elementary school wasn't much better. I still struggled to make friends and rarely spoke up or joined in. From kindergarten through sixth grade, I managed to make a handful of friends, though not many close ones. For the most part, I remained withdrawn. Other kids could be cruel; if you acted differently, they'd quickly label you "weird" or "gay." My choice to wear sweatpants and sweatshirts every single day didn't help, it only fueled their judgments.

Still, I did have a few bright spots in those years: Jen, Whitney, Jason, and Brad. They were my closest friends, the ones who made elementary school far more bearable. Brad was my best friend, the anchor in those uncertain years. I also had some wonderful teachers who helped me navigate school and made it manageable. Academics were never the issue for me, it was always the social side of things. I remember those teachers vividly: Mrs. Coon, Mrs. Derf, Mrs. Rennison, Mrs. Brewer, Mrs. Martin, and Mr. Starkey. I think they sensed how much I struggled to fit in and went out of their way to make me feel comfortable in a world where I had no idea how to be comfortable in my own skin.

Sometimes I wonder how I even made it through elementary school. I definitely had my share of struggles. Maybe "struggles" were just part of my normal. One of the biggest ones was swimming.

Every other nine weeks, our class had to cross the big parking lot between the elementary school and the high school for PE, which was swimming. My fear of swimming had started before I was even in school. My parents tried swim lessons, but I would scream and cry in the water. There's even a home video of me at a private lesson: I'm standing in the pool, crying as the instructor gently tried to coax me into putting my face in the water. It's embarrassing to watch now. I can't fully remember what I felt in that moment, but watching it back still stirs up something heavy in me.

Fast forward to elementary school, and nothing had changed. I was still crying at PE in the swimming pool. Sometimes I worked myself up so badly that I felt physically sick. Sick enough that people thought I had some sort of stomach condition. On swimming days, I'd often beg to see the nurse, complaining of stomach pain. I remember feeling like I might throw up at any moment. I carried this strange fear that I'd vomit in front of everyone at school. And I can still recall, vividly, every single time a classmate actually did throw up in class. Andy, Melinda, and Brian, to name a few.

But something was clearly wrong with me. On swim days, I would make myself sick, every single time. The teacher would eventually send me to the nurse. Finally, my mom caught on and sent Mylanta, that chalky white stomach medicine, instructing the nurse to give it to me and send me straight back to swimming. Those were the days when the school nurse could hand out anything parents provided.

Looking back, I think my struggles really began in elementary school. I barely got through the swimming ordeal, but there was more. When I dug deeper into my memories, I recalled another difficult period: fourth grade. This time, it wasn't about swimming. After Christmas break, I started sobbing in class, for reasons I couldn't explain. What did the other kids think? A fourth-grade boy crying? What a loser, I thought.

Mrs. Martin was my fourth-grade teacher, and she was wonderful. She often read her favorite books aloud, and I loved every minute of it. Which made it all the stranger when I broke down in her classroom. Eventually, she sent me to the school counselor. I can't remember her name, but as a kid, I thought she was odd. Maybe it was just because I had never spoken to anyone about my emotions before. Sitting with her felt uncomfortable, unnatural. I hated it. I'd cry, she'd ask questions, and I'd mumble answers. She wanted to know why I was upset, what was going on in my life. Maybe this was my first real symptom of depression, who knows? She never mentioned the word, and I doubt she was allowed to.

What I remember most is sitting on a beanbag in her dim office, lit only by an orange lamp. It was tucked inside the library, and I always worried other kids or teachers might peek in. She eventually called my parents. When they found out, I felt ashamed, ashamed of crying, ashamed of being sad, ashamed of being found out at all. From then on, I knew I had to bury my feelings deeper and deeper, push them further down where no one could see.

In the end, it turned out I simply missed my mom. Coming back after Christmas break was harder than I expected. Maybe I feared losing her, after all, she had a brain tumor. Maybe that was the start of my hidden depression, disguised as another kind of sadness.

Elementary school wrapped up in a lukewarm way, nothing terrible, nothing amazing. By the time I entered junior high and high school, I felt a little more comfortable in my own skin. I became a varsity athlete, both a runner and, believe it or not, a varsity swimmer. After all those tearful elementary swim lessons and trips to the nurse, I ended up on the swim team. Every year after the season, I received the "Most Improved" award, and Coach Taylor would retell the story of me crying during swim class in grade school. I didn't mind, it actually made me proud. I had overcome that fear of water.

I think I was a happy teenager. Academically, school was easy for me, but socially, it was tough. Don't most teens have angst during those years? I didn't like most of the kids at my school and didn't care to hang out with them. Some assumed I was stuck up or thought I was better than everyone else, but that wasn't true. I just never fit well socially.

I did have a few solid friends: Freddie, Brad, and Robby. We did the classic teenager stuff. I had a two-door blue Blazer, and we'd pile into it and drive to the Applebee's in Crawfordsville, Indiana. With the windows rolled down, we'd blast Ludacris and DMX, passing around a bottle of Southern Comfort. I never drank any being the driver, I didn't dare, but my friends did. My parents would have killed me if they knew. We even sang along to Luda's "You Da Hoe." What a ridiculous song, I can't believe I ever sang it. I hid that CD in my car and never told my parents about either the music or the alcohol. If they had found out, they would have been furious.

Looking back, maybe that's where the demon of depression started to creep in. I've always believed that what you let in is what eventually comes out. And I was letting in a lot of junk. I fed myself awful music and dark media. As a teenager, I was obsessed with horror movies. It's strange because my mom never allowed them in the house, but I always found a way to watch. Scream, the remake of Texas Chainsaw Massacre, you name it, I watched it. At the time, I loved them. Now, I see them as garbage that opened doors I wish I had kept closed. They let fear, even evil, creep into my life.

And fear was always there, hovering over me. Especially at night. Even as a teenager, I was terrified of a home invasion. I'd lie awake imagining someone breaking in, taking us hostage. That fear never really left, it was a constant presence in the background of my life.

Looking back, that constant fear now feels irrational, yet I wonder if it was the seed of the anxiety and depression that would eventually overwhelm me. I wish I had recognized it earlier and found a way to prevent the breakdown that surfaced later in adulthood.

College, by contrast, was filled with joy. I can't pinpoint any clear signs of depression during those years. I loved life in Bloomington, though I completely stopped going to church. Perhaps that distance from my faith was part of my eventual unraveling. I lived a lifestyle that didn't honor God, and in hindsight, I wonder if that opened the door for struggles down the road.

Even in Florida, during my first years as a teacher, I was still mostly happy. The work was difficult, and there were days I hated it, but overall, life seemed manageable. What I did wrestle with was homesickness. Most weekends during those first few months, I'd sit alone, drinking an entire bottle of Chandon while Maroon 5 played on my iPod through a Bose SoundDock until I drifted off to sleep. Eventually, I made some good friends, Brandon, Shawna, and Autumn, and life in Lakeland became easier.

At that time, I wasn't close to God. My faith only began to return when I met my future wife, Kerri. I even found happiness during my early years as an administrator. But when I became principal of an elementary school, the shadows of depression and anxiety grew heavier. I didn't see it for what it was. I thought sadness was just part of the stress of being a principal. The demands of the role were overwhelming at times, and I often grew frustrated with the needless drama among adults in the building. Still, this wasn't just ordinary job stress; there was a deeper, darker sense of oppression woven into the atmosphere of that school, one I couldn't shake.

There was a strange, almost suffocating presence on campus, something dark that seemed to steal the air from my lungs. Each day, I struggled to make sense of what was happening, both in my own mind and in the hearts of my staff and students. It felt as if the oppression leapt from one person to another, spreading like a shadow.

Some teachers, I began to notice, had not only lost their passion for teaching but, even more troubling, their empathy for the children they were meant to serve. It was a sobering realization: not everyone in education was motivated by a love for nurturing young minds. A few had grown bitter and resentful, and their treatment of students reflected it. The hard truth was that some should never have been in the classroom at all. Perhaps the weight of that same oppression had settled on them, twisting their hearts and draining their compassion.

I wrestled daily with these toxic attitudes and the question of how to confront them. What made it worse was the union's protection of these teachers, which only deepened the turmoil. The system seemed built to shield adults rather than prioritize children, and that burden fell heavily on me as I tried to keep students first. The environment became poisonous, and the sense of powerlessness fed my anxiety, tightening the grip of depression that already surrounded me.

Reflecting on these experiences, I realize that depression often hides behind other masks in men, causing them to question themselves or blame outside circumstances. It is a quiet enemy, taking many different shapes, and often remains unnoticed until its weight becomes too heavy to bear.

For me, it took months of inner torment before I began to recognize that I was battling depression. I examined every possible explanation for what I was going through. At first, I became my own doctor, spending endless hours researching symptoms online, turning to "Dr. Google" for answers. Eventually, I visited my primary physician and met with a few therapists. Yet I resisted receiving an official diagnosis. Part of me feared what that label might mean for my life, and I wanted to protect certain personal freedoms that I felt could be threatened by being formally identified as depressed. I know that may sound unreasonable, but at the time, it mattered deeply to me.

In the next chapter, I will share how God began guiding me toward healing through therapy, antidepressants, and His power. Slowly, I started to make sense of what was happening and to step into the long road toward recovery. Facing the truth required peeling back layers of denial and confronting the real nature of my inner struggle. Only then could I begin the difficult journey toward healing and, in time, discover the strength to stand against the oppressive forces that had surrounded me.

—◦◊◦—

CHAPTER 8

Tango with Treatment: Lexapro, Wellbutrin, and the Quest for Stability

In the dimly lit room of my soul, I found myself standing at a crossroads, confronted with the daunting decision of turning to medication for my relentless depression. I had reached the end of my road. It felt as though the path had carried me straight to the edge of a cliff, where a massive drop loomed before me. I had been standing there for what felt like forever, inching my toes closer and closer to the edge. Now, they dangled over, held back only by the weight in my heels. Teetering, swaying, I knew that if I leaned forward, there would be no turning back. The thought of free-falling into the abyss below almost seemed like release, an escape from the thoughts that tormented me. But the grim reality was that the fall itself would plunge me into an even greater hell, one far worse than the pain I was already living through.

I knew I had to fight to shift my weight back to solid ground. I had been seeing a therapist, but earlier that year I quit. I was tired of pouring my heart out to a stranger, only to feel like I was holding back anyway. That relationship felt pointless, so I ended it. Left with few options, I turned to my primary doctor. Quietly, without telling anyone, I scheduled an appointment through the MyChart app because I couldn't bear to talk to anyone about it. When the day finally came, I walked into the office carrying an indescribable sense of shame. At that point, no one in my life knew I was struggling with depression   except the therapist I had already walked away from.

When the doctor asked what was going on, I froze. How could I sum up the worst months of my life to someone who barely knew me? After what felt like an eternity of silence, I finally cleared my throat and spoke the words I had never dared to say out loud: "I think I'm depressed."

The room went quiet. That was all I said. Just five words. But for me, they carried the weight of everything I had been holding in. I had never admitted it to anyone, not even to myself. The doctor looked at me for a moment and simply said, "Okay." No judgment. No shock. Just calm acceptance. Then, almost effortlessly, we shifted into a conversation about medicine.

Inside, I was torn. Part of me wondered, Will I be officially crazy if I start taking medicine? But deep down, I knew I needed something more than whiskey to numb the pain, and I wasn't about to take anything illegal. The doctor explained several options, walking me through how each medication worked, from the heavier hitters to the lighter choices. Prozac. Zoloft. Even Xanax. After much thought, I settled on Lexapro, hoping it would finally give me the relief I had been chasing for so long. I just wanted to feel better. I wanted to climb out of the fog that had suffocated me.

Still, embarrassment lingered. Picking up that prescription felt like wearing a sign around my neck. As I walked into the pharmacy, I was convinced everyone was staring, silently labeling me. When I gave the technician my name, I prayed she wouldn't know what Lexapro was for. She handed me the small bottle, and I quickly paid, refusing the pharmacist's offer to explain the medication. Walking out, I felt a strange mix of shame and hope. For the first time, I was officially a man on meds.

I didn't think it was possible, but Lexapro brought a sense of stability to my restless mind. The chaos of my thoughts began to soften into something more harmonious, and for the first time in a long while, I caught glimpses of the person I used to be.

I started with a half-pill on a Saturday, then increased to a full dose three days later. By day seven, I was stunned by the difference. I remember laughing for no reason, a welcome contrast to all the times I had cried for no reason. I wasn't sure I even remembered what it felt like to laugh, to genuinely laugh. It felt almost foreign, yet freeing. My mood, anger, and irritation finally began to level out. The irrational thoughts were still there, but the medicine gave me the pause I needed to push them aside. For the first time in months, it felt like the old me was resurfacing.

For the next several months, I continued on Lexapro, gradually increasing to my final dose. Happiness felt strange, almost suspicious. I would catch myself laughing and think, Did that really just happen? Just weeks before turning forty, I found myself daring to want company again. For so long, I had wanted nothing more than to isolate, to lock myself away like Howard Hughes. But this time, I asked for a party. My wife threw a murder mystery dinner at our home, surrounded by our closest friends. That night, I felt something I hadn't felt in a year: I felt good. It was one of the best nights I could remember, a small pinhole of light breaking through the tunnel that had trapped me for so long.

But the symphony of relief carried a heavy cost. The side effects came creeping in, the most devastating being sexual dysfunction. I hate admitting it, even now, but it struck at the core of my identity and confidence. I tried to ignore it, to push through, but the problem only grew heavier with time. Mentally, I was thriving; physically, I was unraveling. For men, this kind of struggle is its own quiet nightmare, one that weighs heavily on mental health in ways no one likes to talk about.

And as if that wasn't enough, the weight started piling on. I hadn't expected Lexapro to make me gain so much. The pinhole of light that had seemed so close began to narrow, the tunnel walls closing in around me once again.

As I weighed the benefits against the challenges, the decision to switch medications became unavoidable. I went back to my doctor and, with no small amount of embarrassment, admitted the struggles I was having with intimacy. He confirmed what I already feared: sexual dysfunction is one of the most common side effects of Lexapro, especially for men. We talked through alternatives, each with its own risks and rewards. Desperate both mentally and physically, I agreed to try something new.

We switched to Wellbutrin. Unfortunately, it never fit me the way Lexapro had. In fact, it felt like the opposite of what I needed. Coming off Lexapro was an ordeal in itself. I tapered off slowly, as directed, but it still left me feeling as though my brain was hooked to an electrical current. Every few minutes, I'd get hit with a jolt like a zap shooting through my head. Each zap was paired with a strange falling sensation and a whooshing sound that seemed to echo inside my skull. I'd turn my head, "whoosh." I'd look up, "whoosh." Side to side, "whoosh." It was unnerving, and it lasted for weeks.

After a few months on Wellbutrin, it became clear that it wasn't working. The depression crept back in, sadness, irritation, anger, resentment, all of it. What I did like, though, was that my libido returned. But that came with its own cruel twist: while my body was ready, my mind was still buried in depression. Who wants to be intimate with someone who's angry, irritable, and miserable, which only made the depression worse.

Navigating the transition between medications turned into a frustrating process of trial and error. I tried adjusting the Wellbutrin dosage, but no matter how I increased it, the relief never came. The lift I once felt with Lexapro was nowhere to be found. It became clear how complicated medication management really was, and how important it was to have my doctor guiding me through each step.

Eventually, I went back to him and laid it out plainly: Wellbutrin wasn't working. I asked what else could be done. He suggested, "Why don't we add Lexapro to the Wellbutrin?" I was surprised but willing. At that point, I was desperate for something to break through the fog. Time felt like it was slipping away, and I was beginning to understand how depression could drive people toward dark and irreversible choices. My doctor reassured me that I wouldn't have to take both forever, though the timeline was unclear. Still, when we added Lexapro back in, everything changed. That combination finally gave me the relief I had been searching for. For the first time in a long while, the tiny pinhole of light at the end of the tunnel started to widen.

Alongside medication, I also gave therapy a try. I began with virtual sessions, hoping the digital connection would help, but after five attempts, it felt empty and detached. Craving something deeper, I switched to in-person therapy, where I uncovered old wounds from my past. But after four months, progress seemed to stall, and I reluctantly decided to stop. I don't discourage anyone else from pursuing therapy; it just didn't feel right for me at this stage. Maybe down the road I'll revisit it and dig into my childhood more, but for now, it's on pause.

Desperate for a spark of creativity and self-discovery, I returned to the familiar comfort of my childhood, the piano. I had been classically trained since the age of six, often playing hymns at church whenever Cindy, our regular pianist, wasn't there. My family cherished songs like How Great Thou Art, Wonderful Words of Life, The Old Rugged Cross, and Just as I Am. Those melodies carried echoes of warmth and faith.

With Chopin as my guide, I rediscovered the therapeutic power of music. I set my sights on mastering his Prelude in E Minor, a piece steeped in shadow and emotion. To me, it sounded like a man wrestling with a demon in his soul, struggling until the final, heavy chords. The music mirrored my own fight through darkness. Sitting at the piano, my hands pressing the deep bass notes with careful rhythm, I poured my turmoil into the keys. Each phrase released a piece of the weight I carried, and when the last notes faded, I felt a wave of relief, sometimes with tears streaming down my face.

At the same time, I found another outlet in the vivid colors of abstract painting. Though I had never been especially artistic, aside from a single pottery class in high school, I surrendered to the unpredictability of oil paints. What began as dark, heavy images gradually became a way to untangle my emotions. Regardless of the colors or the chaos that came out on canvas, painting gave me a sense of calm. It became another release, another way of quieting the noise inside me. And to this day, I still find peace standing in front of a blank canvas, brush in hand.

As my journey unfolded, I began to see my healing as a symphony with many movements. The Lord conducted each part, guiding the wisdom of doctors, the use of medicine, and the unexpected therapy of artistic expression. Though my path was far from ordinary, I learned to embrace the harmony of treatment, faith, and self-discovery, finding peace in the notes of restoration.

CHAPTER 9

Emerging from the Shadows:
A Journey Toward Light

As I sat alone in a dimly lit room, weighed down by the suffocating grip of my thoughts, I couldn't escape the feeling that everything was my fault. Guilt pressed on me like a heavy blanket, each moment adding another layer to the despair that covered my soul. I told myself, Of course, Ryan, it's your fault. You've treated people poorly, you've been harsh. It's easy to accept the verdict the world often gives: when a man struggles, he is the one to blame. But I wondered if we could look deeper? Could we search for the roots of the pain before dismissing the man altogether?

In the depths of depression, I felt trapped in a pit of remorse and self-condemnation. Every misstep, every wrong turn echoed endlessly, convincing me I was the sole cause of the darkness. Depression in men can feel like a revolving death cycle: the illness consumes us, we can't escape the shadows, we lash out at those we love, they turn away, and then we sink further into guilt, repeating the spiral again and again. I prayed relentlessly for God to break me free.

And in those darkest moments, a flicker of light pierced through the shadows. It was the whisper of hope, the faint glow at the end of the tunnel. God was answering my prayers, not in my timing, but in His. I began to hear a quiet call toward self-compassion, urging me to release the chains of guilt and embrace forgiveness not only for others but for myself. We serve a God of grace, mercy, and forgiveness. And when I could not forgive myself, He already had.

One of the hardest parts of my journey with depression was carrying the weight of personal forgiveness. I spent countless hours trapped in my own mind, replaying decisions, conversations, and moments I wished I had handled differently. It was as if I stood at the edge of a cliff, watching the stones of my choices tumble into the abyss, convincing myself they had built the very foundation of my depression. I believed I had caused it, my failures, my shortcomings, my inadequacies. I wasn't just battling the crushing sadness that pressed against my chest each morning; I was battling the belief that I deserved it. My mistakes, whether real or imagined, became chains I could not shake.

Forgiving others was difficult, but forgiving myself seemed impossible. It felt like excusing things I couldn't let go of, like betraying the pain I carried so deeply. Each day, the voice of if only haunted me: If only I had been healthier, stronger, kinder, a better Christian. Those words overshadowed the brighter parts of my life, leaving me in constant self-condemnation. No matter how others tried to remind me of my worth, I could not hear them. I had become my own harshest critic, my own jailer, trapped in a prison of shame.

I knew I had to dig deep and begin the journey toward self-forgiveness   something I never thought possible, and certainly not on my own. I found rest in the Lord's guiding hand, which led me to confront the demons of my past and discover the healing power of forgiveness. The task was daunting, laced with pain and uncertainty, but with each step forward the heavy burden of guilt began to lift from my weary soul.

I realized that I couldn't forgive myself until I forgave others. I began with my wife. Deep down, I had felt abandoned by her, and letting go of that wound was the first step. From there, I moved on to many others from my past. I won't go into details here, but I carried far more hurt in my heart than I had ever admitted.

The final and hardest step was turning my forgiveness inward. I looked at my own life honestly, reflecting on the toxic influences I had allowed to shape me. I came to see that what I fed my mind, through the images I watched, the music I absorbed, the voices I let in, had fueled my descent into darkness. Acknowledging that truth was painful, but it was also the beginning of freedom.

The movies filled with awful scenes and the music laced with negative lyrics shaped my mind around a worldly culture rather than a Godly lifestyle. The relentless barrage of darkness only deepened the shadows within me, dragging me further into the abyss. Yet perhaps the most insidious enemy I faced was my own self-pity. I had become skilled at the "woe is me" act. Day by day, I sank deeper into the quicksand of despair, trapped in a vicious cycle of blame and self-recrimination. Every moment spent wallowing in pity only fueled the flames of my depression, leaving me lost and adrift in a sea of hopelessness.

It was only when I mustered the courage to confront my demons, to acknowledge my flaws and imperfections without surrendering to despair, that I began to glimpse light at the end of the tunnel. With each small act of self-compassion, the shadows receded, replaced by glimmers of hope and renewal. The path is not easy, and I still face battles with my demons every day.

Yet as I stand upon the rocks of a new dawn, I am reminded of the power of forgiveness, both for others and for myself. From the prison of suffering, I have learned that true healing begins with a heart unburdened by guilt and regret, illuminated by the light of compassion and grace. Grace that only God can provide. And though the road ahead may be littered with challenges, I now walk it with renewed purpose, strengthened by the assurance that even in the darkest of nights, the dawn of redemption will always break through.

—◦◊◦—

CHAPTER 10

Midnight Mourning:

A Year That Never Came

As the clock struck midnight on New Year's Eve of 2022, I found myself standing in the embrace of darkness, both outside and within. It was a night unlike any other, weighed down by the struggles and burdens I carried. I wanted so badly to believe that when the old year slipped away and the clock turned to 12:00:00 AM, I would be made new. That in a single moment, God would heal my mind.

It felt like the closing chapter of a year that had tested me in ways I could never have imagined. I clung to the hope that with the simple turning of a page, everything would reset, that by the grace of God my spirit would be restored. I gripped that thought with all my might, as though believing could make it true.

Perhaps I was longing for a miracle, a divine intervention that would sweep away the agony I had been drowning in. I wanted to believe God had been watching me, that He had seen my suffering, and that this moment would be the turning point, the fresh start I so desperately craved. After all, we were in church, ushering in the new year with praise and worship.

Yet beneath that fragile hope was a whisper I couldn't silence: What if nothing changed? And when the night ended, my greatest fear became reality. The new year had come, but the healing I prayed for did not.

The church sanctuary, usually glowing with warmth and hope, seemed instead to mirror the desolation of my soul. Dressed in all black, I wore my grief like a shroud, each garment reflecting the pain buried deep within me. My new black spiky shoes mirrored the sharp edges of depression cutting through my spirit, while a black sweater, punk-rock in style with metal zippers running down the sides and a long-line silhouette, hung heavy on me. It wasn't my usual look at all. To complete the outfit, I wore dark, ripped skinny jeans, torn from top to bottom.

It was a far cry from my normal church attire, typically a black blazer with blue jeans. That night, though, I looked more like a member of Green Day than myself. The outfit was more than fashion; it was a testament to the death of joy that had smothered me all year. I was in mourning, mourning my life, my year, the year from hell. My all-black attire was meant as a symbol of heartache, but no one else knew why. I was the only one grieving my life, and no one seemed to notice. Wasn't it obvious I was screaming for help? Yet somehow, my silent cries remained unheard.

Family Worship Center's New Year's Eve gathering was always my favorite. We called it the Agreement Service. As a family, we would write down what we were believing for in the coming year. That night, I knew exactly what I was asking God for: a complete healing of my mind, the death of my broken self, and renewal in my marriage. We still have the flier hanging in our bathroom. In my wife's handwriting, it says: "Restoration in our marriage and peace in our home" and "Anxiety and depression gone."

I remember how difficult it was to ask her to write those words. I softened it to just anxiety and depression, though in truth what I wanted to say was closer to: "Jesus, take away my depression and my desire to leave this life behind. I'm struggling and I can't take another moment of living." But I shortened it to four words.

As we stood together during the service, hands clasped in prayer, I silently begged for relief from the Category 5 storm raging in our lives, something no one else knew about, nor could they understand. Looking back at pictures from that night, I see it written all over my face. I looked terrible. Who was I kidding? Tears welled in my eyes...

Unsolicited, as the pastor's voice filled the sanctuary, a flicker of hope broke through the darkness of my life. He prayed over each family, one by one. Section by section, we lined up and made our way forward. There I stood, in my punk rock shoes, holding my wife's hand as we inched closer. I was sobbing uncontrollably. Even now, as I write this, I can feel those same emotions, the sting of tears rising just as they did that night. It remains fresh, etched into my memory. That moment felt like life or death. I knew I couldn't walk away unchanged.

Finally, we reached the pastor and his wife. Kerri and I held our agreement card together, our hands clasped tightly over it. Everything seemed to move in slow motion as Pastor Shawn and Abigail placed their hands on ours. Tears streamed down my face. The pastor prayed over us as a family, perhaps the most prayer I had ever received during my battle with depression. His touch, his words, carried a plea for renewal and agreement. Yet beneath it all, I felt the weight of my anguish pressing against me like a lead cloak.

When our turn ended, we walked back to our seats. I was still crying, though I tried to contain it. We moved up the far stage-right aisle, then across the main center row. I wiped my tears quickly, desperate to hold together the fragile façade of happiness.

How could I embrace the promise of a new year when the shadows of the past clung to me with relentless weight? Ringing in the year was nothing like I had hoped. The countdown felt as though it moved in slow motion. Around me, everyone was celebrating, singing, praising, rejoicing, while I pushed forward, desperate just to cross into the new year.

When the glittering "2022" and the bursts of pyrotechnics faded into memory, I was left with the same painful truth: God had not healed me in that instant. I was still mourning my broken, depressed life. I had hoped to walk out of the sanctuary a new man, freed from despair in the blink of God's power. And yes, God is powerful enough to heal in a moment, but that was not His plan for my journey. My healing would not be instant. Instead, all I could see ahead was a barren stretch of days, a wilderness of uncertainty and pain. I wondered if I would have to wait until another New Year's Eve to feel whole again.

Nine long months passed before the dawn of something new, nine months of darkness, despair, and relentless battles within my mind. Yet even in the turmoil, I clung to fragile threads of hope, faint glimmers of light that refused to die out. As I struggled through, I discovered strength I didn't know I had: the strength to endure, to persevere against the tide of depression that kept pressing in. The road ahead was still filled with challenges, but with faith as my compass, I trusted that I could survive even the darkest nights and, in time, step into the light of a new day.

CHAPTER 11

Finding Light:

Reclaiming Joy

There was a season in my life when joy felt like nothing more than a distant memory, always just beyond my grasp. I longed to hold it again, but it slipped away like a dream I could no longer recall. I knew I had once been full of joy, but the when and how of it had vanished, leaving only a hollow void that seemed impossible to fill. The absence of joy weighed heavily on my heart and mind, casting shadows across every corner of my existence. I began to wonder if life without joy was even worth continuing.

Depression became my constant companion, clinging to me day and night, suffocating me in both the brightness of morning and the darkness of evening. It consumed everything, swallowing what little happiness remained and replacing it with despair. I had lived so long without joy that I began to wonder whether I even knew how to live with it anymore. Each day was a battle with this relentless enemy, one that threatened to push me to the brink of ending it all.

One sweltering summer afternoon, I stepped out onto the patio by my pool, laptop in hand, hoping the fresh air might ease my mind. But there was no breeze   only thick, stifling heat. The stillness around me mirrored the stillness within me. I longed for even the faintest wind of joy, but it never came. I sat at the table staring at the water, imagining what it would be like to dive in, sink to the bottom, and never come back up. No one would be there to pull me out. The thought became a haunting metaphor for my life, drowning in silence, unseen and unheard.

I was dying inside, yet no one could hear my silent cries for rescue from this beast called depression. By God's grace, I never acted on those dark thoughts, but the weight of life pressed on me with unbearable force. Emptiness gnawed at my spirit. I felt surrounded by the enemy, convinced that joy had abandoned me and that I was utterly alone. The lie took hold so strongly that I began to believe not even God could help me. My mental health crumbled under the pressure, leaving me lost, broken, and unsure if I could ever be restored.

I searched desperately for a way out of the darkness, clinging to the hope that somewhere, somehow, a small glimmer of light might guide me through the storm. Yet joy remained out of reach, hidden beneath the weight of my emotions. The path forward was unclear, blurred by pain and uncertainty.

In those darkest moments, I turned once again to my faith, seeking refuge in the promises of the Lord. Deep within, I knew that true joy could only come from Him, that He alone held the key to unlocking the prison of my despair. So I immersed myself in His Word, searching for timeless truths that could reach the far corners of my weary soul. Through scripture, faint sparks of hope began to appear, tiny flickers of joy pushing back against the shadows.

The journey, however, was anything but easy. There were days when I felt utterly lost, when the words of the Bible blurred into nothing more than a jumble of letters. At times, the enemy clouded my mind, distorting the truth. Some days I couldn't even find the strength to pray, the weight of depression pressing too heavily on my chest. Slowly, I came to realize a simple but profound truth: God was with me. He had a plan. And though I wanted His plan to be quick and painless, He was choosing to lead me through the fire instead of plucking me out of it. I learned to keep my eyes fixed on what lay beyond the flames, trusting that He would carry me through.

Even in my weakest moments, I knew I had to keep pressing forward, reaching for His light even when it seemed impossibly distant. I began to pray wherever I was: my car, my couch, my office, sometimes in words, sometimes in the Spirit. I would cry out: "Lord, I thank You for this life You've given me. I pray today that this burden of depression would be lifted from my soul and that Your grace would cover me while I wait. In Jesus's name, Amen."

Gradually, almost imperceptibly, something began to shift within me. I sensed the stirrings of a presence greater than myself, a whisper of grace breathing life into my weary spirit. In moments of surrender, I tasted a peace beyond understanding, a joy that welled up from deep inside my soul. It was not an instant transformation   there were setbacks, days when the darkness closed in again, when despair tugged at me like a fierce wind pulling me away from truth. At times, it felt like being trapped in a cellar with the door torn off, a violent storm trying to drag me into oblivion.

But even through those storms, I clung to God's promise that joy would come in the morning, that He would not leave me comfortless. I held tight to His Word and His promises, refusing to let go. And slowly, the clouds began to part, revealing the radiant light of His love shining upon me.

I learned that He is the very source of joy. Joy is not just an emotion, it is a state of being, a choice we must embrace each day, and a gift that only comes from Him. God Himself is our joy. The journey is not easy, but it is a pilgrimage of the soul that draws us closer to the One who is the wellspring of all fulfillment.

As I look back on those dark, heavy days, I am overwhelmed with gratitude for the journey that has brought me here. My eyes still fill with tears when I remember those moments, but they are tears of both sorrow and thankfulness. I am thankful that I am no longer trapped there, and I am in awe of the beauty that can rise from the ashes of hopelessness, of the joy that can spring forth from the deepest sorrow. Like a diamond formed in fire, my pain has been refined into something greater.

Above all, I am reminded that true joy comes only from the Lord. He alone has the power to transform our deepest wounds into our greatest triumphs. In Him, I have discovered the joy I once believed was lost forever, a joy without limits, a joy that nothing can take away.

My prayer is that we would all find the courage to seek joy in our darkest hours, to trust the light that shines even when shadows seem unending. For in the presence of the Lord, joy is always waiting to be found. If only we hold on in faith and believe.

CHAPTER 12

The Journey of Regret:

The Struggles of a Husband and Father

In the spiral of my despair, I felt as though I were drowning in an endless sea of darkness, struggling to live up to the roles of husband and father that both society and my own expectations had placed upon me. Depression settled over me like a suffocating fog, consuming every thought and leaving me unable to meet even the most basic responsibilities at home. At times, I doubted I could even keep myself safe. The weight of it pressed so heavily on me that I wondered if my family would be better off without me. How could I possibly protect my wife and daughter when I could not find the strength to carry myself through the day?

I remember sitting alone, tears streaming down my face, clinging to the words of 1 Corinthians 13: "Love is kind." I read those words again and again, each syllable cutting through the haze of hopelessness, though unable to fully pierce the depths of my soul. Anger, frustration, and helplessness consumed me, and I convinced myself that I alone had to find a way to change the broken narrative of my life.

As depression tightened its grip, I withdrew further from the sanctuary of my home. Tasks that once came easily now felt unbearable. My wife, the steady rock in my storms, watched with aching eyes as I slipped deeper into the shadows. Helpless, she saw me retreat into myself, unable to muster the strength to load the dishwasher, let alone share in the daily rhythms of the life we once built together.

A clear sign for my wife came when I stopped unloading the dishwasher. That small task had always been mine, but as sorrow consumed me, I left it untouched and she noticed. I hated life. I hated home. I hated the very essence of an existence that weighed so heavily on my shoulders. And in that hatred, I unknowingly wounded the very people I loved most.

My daughter, innocent and pure, bore the brunt of my anguish. She felt the sharp edge of my attitude and the weight of my discontent. I was a terrible father in those moments, lost in my own darkness and unable to see past the shadows clouding my mind. I was still a new dad. My daughter was only four years old, and fatherhood was not unfolding the way I had imagined. Not that it's easy for anyone, but I thought I would thrive. Instead, depression turned me into someone I barely recognized. I was present in body but absent in spirit, a million miles away from her.

I'll never forget one morning during the first few months of my depression. My wife was out of town, and it fell on me to get our daughter ready for preschool. It was a Friday. I dragged myself out of bed, though every fiber of me longed to stay under the covers. Still, I knew I had to step up as her father. When I woke her, she was burning with fever. Immediately, I knew something was wrong. I gave her Tylenol and called my wife, because isn't that what good husbands do? She told me to wait for the medicine to work and check again.

But the fever didn't break. It climbed to 102.5, and panic overwhelmed me. My hatred for life clouded my judgment, and I couldn't think clearly. I called my wife again, sobbing uncontrollably. It's hard to admit the shame of that moment, me, sitting on the cold tile floor of our living room at seven in the morning, breaking down on the phone while my sick daughter watched. Her temperature kept rising, and I knew I had to take her to the ER. At first, I felt paralyzed, completely unfit for the task.

Somehow, I gathered enough strength to get her there. Sitting in that emergency room, I asked myself over and over: How can I make this work? How can I truly be the father my daughter needs?

My wife also carried the weight of my inadequacy. I could see it etched in the furrow of her brow and the weariness in her eyes. She longed for the husband she once knew, the partner who shared in life's joys and burdens with devotion. But I had become only a shadow of that man, trapped in the maze of my mind, unable to find my way back to the light.

Even in my lowest moments, I couldn't shake the belief that men are rarely given grace when it comes to mental health. Society expects us to be unshakable pillars of strength, the anchors our families depend on. Our wives and children look to us for stability. But when the cracks begin to show, when the weight becomes unbearable, we often stand alone, abandoned by those who once leaned on us. The world turns its back on men struggling with depression, and painfully, my wife was no different.

The thought of my marriage falling apart only deepened the darkness. I believe in the sanctity of marriage, in the sacred bond between husband and wife that is meant to endure life's storms. Yet I also believe in the power of partnership, in the mutual support needed when confusion and uncertainty press in. Scripture teaches that a man is to lead his home, but even the strongest leaders need a steady hand to guide them through the storm.

In my darkest hours, when the weight of life pressed so heavily I could scarcely breathe, I longed for escape, a brief reprieve from the relentless agony that consumed me. Better death than this, I told myself, unwilling to endure the crushing sense of inadequacy any longer. Yet even within the shadows of despair, a fragile spark endured: a glimmer of hope, a whisper of possibility that would not be extinguished. For even in the prison of suffering, among the ashes of broken wishes and dreams, I discovered the transformative power of love, a love patient and kind, a love that endures even the blackest night. It was not the fleeting love of the world but the steadfast love of God, descending upon me. With that love, I found the courage to believe in redemption, in healing, in a future wrested from the jaws of misery.

CHAPTER 13

The Breakthrough:

Experiencing the Power of Redemption

As I sit down to write this chapter, I'm struck by the weight of time. It's been over a year since the darkness first descended, wrapping its suffocating grip around my soul. More than 365 days since depression began to haunt my every waking moment. I've spent months wrestling with emotions ranging from numbness to despair, from fleeting glimpses of hope to the crushing weight of sadness pressing in from all sides.

There have been countless long days filled with dread and intrusive thoughts thoughts about leaving this Earth. A full year of something I never imagined could happen to me. Over 365 days trapped inside what feels like a dead soul, slowly decaying.

As I reflect on this moment, though, I hesitate to call it a "milestone", perhaps it's better called a setback, or even a regression, I'm confronted with the brutal reality of my journey. It's been a confusing, punishing road, marked by victories and defeats though, honestly, mostly defeats.

Still, there were moments of lightness. Moments when I dared to believe the darkness might be lifting. And yet, more often than not, I found myself back in its grip, still living under the shadow of relentless sadness. I hesitated to hope, because what if happiness returned, only for the darkness to snuff it out again? That has always been my greatest fear.

And yet, despite the fear, despite the weight of it all, there have been glimmers of light. Pockets of growth. Small victories. Quiet reflections that pointed me back to something bigger than the pain. I've learned to celebrate tiny moments of joy, to practice gratitude, even when it's fleeting.

In all of this, I discovered a resilience I never knew I had, a strength forged in the fire of pain and sorrow. A strength not of my own making. A strength that only God could give. Because only God can pull you back from the ledge of a skyscraper and whisper a reminder of His redeeming power.

There was one pivotal moment, one unmistakable God moment, when He did just that. He shoved me backward before I could jump. It happened on October 23, 2022, a date forever etched in my memory.

It was a crisp fall Sunday. I was standing in church, my heart heavy with the weight of a soul burning under the pressure of depression. Every single day for the past year had felt like this. My spirit was weary. My hope nearly gone.

We were wrapping up the praise and worship set. I can't recall the exact songs we sang that morning, but what I do remember, vividly, is the emptiness. That aching void inside me.

It's hard to explain what it feels like to stand in a church filled with the presence of the Holy Spirit and still feel completely disconnected. The people around me were worshiping, praising, reaching for God with joy and passion, and I forced myself to raise my hands, to at least try. I wanted to feel what they were feeling. I've felt it before, many times, when the Spirit falls. But that morning, something inside me was blocking it.

I felt like a spectator, standing outside of something beautiful and sacred. Watching, but not partaking. There was an invisible barrier between me and the presence that was lifting everyone else. I was stuck, desperate to break through, but unable to move.

As the singing came to a close, Pastor Shawn walked up the steps to the platform, just as he did every Sunday after worship. He began to pray over us while the band played softly behind him. Then, in what could only be described as divine intervention, something unexpected happened.

A man from the congregation suddenly interrupted. Pastor Shawn stopped mid-sentence. The band's drums, guitar, and piano faded into silence. The entire sanctuary went still. All eyes turned toward the source of the interruption: a gray-haired man, likely in his 80s, standing tall as he bellowed a message in tongues.

For those unfamiliar with Spirit-filled churches, this may sound strange. But in the context of spiritual gifts, speaking in tongues is a sacred and intimate form of communication with God. It's not gibberish or noise, it's a divine language, spoken through the prompting of the Holy Spirit. A message in tongues isn't spoken for show; it is a vessel of divine expression, meant to edify, exhort, or comfort those present. In that moment, the speaker becomes a conduit between heaven and earth.

I won't try to write down the untranslated message. But I still hear it in my spirit. I still feel what it did to me. At FWC, we believe in the gifts God gives His people, and this man had the gift of prophesying in tongues. As he spoke, I felt the sound pierce straight into my soul.

It was as if I opened my mouth and the darkness screamed out of me. It escaped like a storm breaking free. It felt like a lightning bolt hit me. I raised my hands to heaven, knowing this message, though still unintelligible, was for me.

A message in tongues often comes with a call for interpretation. Without the gift of understanding, the message remains hidden. But when interpreted, it bypasses the intellect and reaches the spirit. It shakes something loose. It exposes truth. It brings healing, clarity, and conviction. It's a reminder that God speaks beyond our language, but always with purpose: to guide, to heal, to restore.

There I stood, hands raised, eyes closed. And in that moment, it felt like I was the only one in the room. Everything else faded away. The Holy Spirit surrounded me. It was peace, real peace, right in the heart of my darkness.

After a moment of stillness, Pastor Reggie walked slowly up the stairs. He took the microphone and began to speak with confidence and calm. He delivered the interpretation of the message.

And the words... They cut through the darkness like a shaft of light.

> "For the season that you are in is a season that will pass. Just know that I am in the season with you, and nothing you are facing will last. Come and lift up your voice and give Him praise, for He is good."

Pastor Reggie stepped down from the platform, returned the microphone, and made his way back to his seat. The entire moment unfolded in slow motion for me. My hands were still lifted, and tears streamed down my face as I exhaled a long, trembling breath, like I'd been holding it through the sacred stillness between the tongues and the interpretation.

Those translated words struck with a heavenly certainty, a certainty only God could give. And in that moment, something inside me shifted. It felt like the very air was charged with divine electricity. The Spirit fell on me for the first time in a long time and I felt Him. Not as an idea, not as a memory, but as a presence. Tangible. Real. Near.

I knew, deep in my bones, that the message was for me. It wasn't generic encouragement, it was God's direct word of hope and affirmation. His way of saying, I have not left you.

Redemption touched me in that moment.

And in the heart of the darkness, I felt it: the static spark of hope. A flicker of light breaking through the weight. A pulse of life in the middle of spiritual silence. I don't remember the rest of the church service at all. I couldn't tell you what the sermon was about or where we went to eat afterward. I left the building with my family and spent the rest of the day in a haze.

The moment I got home, I grabbed my phone and pulled up the live stream of the 9 a.m. service. I played that moment over and over again, bursting into tears each time. I'm sure they were happy tears, or maybe tears of release, tears that understood the weight of the words spoken and the redemption carried within them.

I screen-recorded the clip on my phone, capturing every word, every pause, every nuance of that divine utterance. I wanted it all. The dramatic stillness after the message in tongues. Pastor Shawn standing on stage, hands cupped over his mouth, soaking it in. Pastor Reggie rising from his seat, grabbing a microphone, and walking up to interpret.

I needed to preserve every syllable of that moment.

In the days and weeks that followed, I watched that video again and again   sometimes late at night, sometimes first thing in the morning. I drew strength from it. Comfort. Solace. It became my lifeline, a divine reminder that even in the pitch-black night, there is always a flicker of light, if only we have the eyes to see it.

Armed with this rediscovered hope, I believed, maybe for the first time in a long while, that I could claw my way out of the pit. It wasn't easy. Far from it. There were days when the darkness returned with a vengeance. Days when the pain felt unbearable. When it felt like too much to keep going.

But through it all, I clung to that word like a drowning man clings to a life raft   desperate, breathless, but still holding on.

That word was my lifeline.

My reminder.

My rescue.

My Savior from above.

Looking back now, I realize that it was this moment, the moment when the man spoke in tongues and Pastor Reggie interpreted, that marked the beginning of my journey back to myself. It was like watching a crash test in slow motion. I was the car, speeding toward a concrete wall. I hit it, shattered on impact... and bounced back. Slower. Broken. But healing.

That moment was the turning point. The catalyst for change I had desperately needed. And though I knew the road ahead would be long and full of obstacles, something inside me had shifted. I understood, finally, that I was not alone. In fact, I never had been.

God had been there through it all. He was pulling me out of the muck and mire of depression. He was saving my life.

In the months that followed, subtle changes began to take root. My perspective started to shift. Tiny flashes of light began breaking through the fog. Do I dare say it? I started to feel joy again: in the laughter of my wife and daughter, in the colors of a sunrise, in the gentle touch of a warm breeze on my skin.

The sadness didn't disappear. It lingered, like a shadow I couldn't fully shake but it no longer defined me. I found peace in knowing that I wasn't alone. That I could be redeemed. That there was a purpose to my pain, and a reason for my suffering. God was redeeming me and keeping me on this Earth for a reason. My life wasn't meant to be hell on Earth. And my eternity wasn't going to be hell either. So now, as I write these words, tears stream down my face, not from sorrow, but from gratitude.

Gratitude for the journey.

For the lessons.

For the grace that carried me through the darkest of nights.

For His redemptive power.

And though the road ahead is still long, and uncertainty still waits around every corner, I am comforted by the One who walks beside me.

The God who gave those prophetic words so many months ago.

The God who is still with me, guiding me, sustaining me, and leading me ever onward… into the light.

⸺◦◊◦⸺

CHAPTER 14

Deserted by Many,

Embraced by God

In the deep sea of depression, when the world seemed to shrink away and relationships felt like shadowy figures just above the water and out of reach, I found myself floating, alone. Abandoned by most, but not by God.

Have you ever been to the bottom of a lake or the ocean? As you sink deeper and deeper, the light fades. Everything above you becomes distorted, hard to recognize. The silence becomes deafening. That's how my life felt: disoriented, isolated, lost in the cold, crushing pressure of despair.

Social isolation had taken hold of me completely. And while I've always been an introvert, someone who genuinely enjoys time alone, this was different. This isolation wasn't peaceful. It was suffocating. It left me alone with the darkest corners of my mind. And in those moments of silence, the only voices I could hear were cruel. Dark thoughts ran wild, questions that no one should ever have to face.

Looking back, I wish I had reached out to friends or family sooner. But pride had built a wall, and resentment held it in place. I bottled everything up and kept my mouth shut. My first real confession didn't come in a conversation, it came in a Facebook post.

Wow. What a mistake.

The post is long gone now, deleted forever, but I still cringe when I think about it. I don't even remember what it said exactly. Something like, "I've been depressed, and I'm struggling."

I guess part of me wanted people to know. Maybe I was hoping for sympathy. Or understanding. Or just to shake off the label of being cold, angry, or distant. I wanted to explain the unexplainable, and in my desperation, I dumped it on social media. People commented. And for a few seconds, maybe it felt nice. But then my wife and my mom saw it.

That's when everything went sideways.

My mom had no idea what I was going through. She was hurt. It felt to her like I had told the whole world before I told her, and in a way, I had. What she didn't know, what no one knew, was that I hadn't told anyone. Everyone found out at the same time, in the same way: publicly and suddenly.

I wanted to open up. But instead, I dropped a bomb. And the people closest to me were left to deal with the fallout. My wife, once my friend, my comforter, turned away, unable to bear the weight of my darkness. I couldn't blame her. Depression is a relentless beast. It devours joy and connection with equal hunger. I couldn't talk to her. She didn't want to talk to me.

Unable to articulate the depths of my torment, I retreated into silence, lying to everyone, my parents, my wife, my friends, insisting I was fine when I was anything but. The fracture in our relationship deepened when she turned to her parents for support, sharing the burden I had tried so hard to hide. Resentment raged through me like a wildfire in Northern California, consuming what little was left of my already broken heart. Maintaining connections felt impossible when the very act of existing felt unbearable.

During this time, I nearly lost her. We were dangerously close to becoming another statistic, another story of love unraveling under the weight of a mental health crisis. It's hard to describe the weight of that realization, to know she may have considered leaving me. At the time, I couldn't see it clearly. I was too trapped in my own darkness, too overwhelmed by pain to see what was slipping through my fingers.

I was consumed by guilt, confusion, and a sense of profound loss, not just of myself, but of us. Now, looking back, I understand why she felt the way she did. Depression wasn't just something I was going through, it was something we were both enduring. It created distance. It stole my ability to show up for her emotionally. Sometimes even physically. I was withdrawn, buried in a world of self-doubt and shame. She had every right to feel frustrated. Every right to be exhausted. Maybe even hopeless. It's incredibly hard to stand by someone who's sinking when you don't have a rope strong enough to pull them back.

But even with that understanding, there's a part of me that still aches, a part that feels betrayed. Because the last thing a man drowning in depression needs is an anchor that walks away. In my lowest moments, I felt abandoned. Like my brokenness was too heavy, even for the person I thought would carry it with me.

I know it's painful to admit, but the truth is this:

Depression is already a lonely battle.

And when the person you love the most considers walking away, it can feel like the final blow. Our vows said "in sickness and in health." But does mental health count in that?

Statistics would later confirm what I had felt all along: depression corrodes relationships, leaving behind a barren landscape of broken bonds and unspoken pain. It's an uphill battle, trying to untangle the knots of your own mind while also reaching for the fading connections around you. And yet, in the wreckage of those relationships, one anchor held firm: the promises of God. In my shattered soul, belief in Jesus Christ lit the way forward. When everything else seemed to fall apart, His presence offered peace. Strength. Hope.

Woven into the teachings of Scripture are promises, unchanging truths that whisper light into chaos. In the pages of the Bible, I found a hiding place from the Category 5 hurricane in my mind. Psalm 34:18 became one of those anchors. A verse I had highlighted in my Bible app, blue, so I'd never forget. I checked the date: April 21, 2022. Ten months into the storm. Still months away from the breakthrough.

> "The LORD is near to the brokenhearted and saves the crushed in spirit." (ESV)

God is omnipresent. Always there. It's a truth I often forgot. A truth I sometimes ignored. But one that never stopped being real. He is near in our brokenness. He restores. The enemy named depression prowled in the shadows of my mind, weaving its suffocating web. But with the Word of God as my weapon, I could stand, sometimes barely, but stand nonetheless.

Ephesians 6:12 also grounded me:

> "For we do not wrestle against flesh and blood, but against the rulers, against the authorities, against the cosmic powers over this present darkness, against the spiritual forces of evil in the heavenly places." (ESV)

This verse reminded me that my battle wasn't against myself. It wasn't even against other people. It was spiritual. Cosmic. Eternal. And the only way to fight a war like that…

Is with God beside you.

The story of Job echoed through the hollowness of my mind, a testament to the enduring nature of faith amid the tempest of despair. Like Job, I grappled with the weight of affliction, surrounded by well-meaning friends whose words offered little comfort and much rebuke. Job's friends spoke against him, talking down to him, unable to comprehend the depths of his pain. In their reflections, I saw my own journey, abandoned and ridiculed by those who couldn't understand my suffering.

Like Job, I found myself going back and forth with friends, especially my wife. I would share my agony, and she would offer her rebuttal, words that cut deeply into an already broken self. I felt condemned, much like Job when Elihu said, "Surely God does not hear an empty cry, nor does the Almighty regard it." (Job 35:13, ESV)

Yet, even in my darkness, the Word of God remained my only

lifeline, a beacon of hope lighting the path to redemption. The LORD spoke to Job and challenged him. He rebuked Job's friends and restored Job's fortunes. He answered Job's prayers and blessed him with twice as much as he had before. His family returned, eating with him, offering comfort and sympathy.

God is restoring me, doubling my good fortune, and blessing my family and generations to come.

In the grip of darkness, I found refuge in the warmth of His promises, weaving His words through my mind, covering me with grace and mercy. Through begging prayers and tear-stained confessions, I discovered the infinite grace of a God who never abandoned me, even within the shadowed walls of depression.

In the end, it was those biblical promises that carried me through the darkest nights, His omnipresence shining brightly amidst the encroaching shadows, a testament to the enduring power of His promises and my unwavering belief in His love.

CHAPTER 15

The Weight of Shame

As a Christian, I once held an unrealistic expectation, that my faith in Christ would shield me from certain struggles. I believed depression should be one of them. I thought if my faith were strong enough and my walk with God close enough, I would be immune to the dark weight that overtook my mind. But when depression hit, it came with a crushing sense of shame, a shame that whispered I had failed, that I wasn't a "good enough" Christian. How could I, a believer, be overwhelmed by something that seemed to contradict everything my faith stood for?

This shame was rooted in the belief that Christians should always be "happy" because of the joy found in Christ. I thought I should be strong and full of faith at all times. What I didn't realize was that no one, not even those who profess faith, is exempt from the struggles of the human condition. Depression is not a failure of faith; it is a part of living in a broken world. Yet, the shame ran deep, convincing me that I was spiritually weak.

But here is the truth I discovered in the darkest depths of my struggle: Jesus alone can remove my shame. No amount of hiding it, fighting it on my own, or pretending it wasn't there could lift the burden I carried. The only remedy was the cross. The same Jesus who bore our sins on Calvary also bore the shame of our past.

When He died, He didn't just take on our guilt, He took on every piece of condemnation, every heavy whisper that says, "You're not enough," "You've failed," "You're too broken." Jesus' death was for all of that. Isaiah 53:4 declares, "Surely he has borne our griefs and carried our sorrows…" (ESV). He was bruised, beaten, and shamed so we wouldn't have to bear it alone. That exchange of His suffering for our freedom is where shame meets its ultimate defeat.

I first gave my life to Christ when I was a kid, ten years old, to be exact. It happened at the small white church in Wallace. I had always believed in Jesus, but that day was the official moment I declared that I knew Jesus died for my sins. At ten, I don't think I fully understood God's love. I didn't realize that Jesus was taking all my guilt from my past. Honestly, I'm not even sure how much guilt I had at that age. I started participating in communion but didn't really get it. I didn't fully grasp that Jesus was bruised, beaten, and shamed for my freedom. It took me years to understand the true meaning of His suffering.

The story of communion reminds us of this incredible exchange. As Christians, when we partake in the bread and the wine, we remember His body broken for us and His blood shed for us. It's a tangible reminder of the price He paid so that we might live in the light of His grace, free from the shame that sin, and yes, even depression, can bring.

Communion isn't just a ritual; it's a declaration. Every time we take it, we proclaim that His sacrifice was enough. We're reminded that faith isn't about being strong on our own but about acknowledging our need for His strength. He didn't ask us to be perfect, only to be His. That's a hard truth for me to fully accept. I was raised to be perfect: the perfect son, the perfect student, the perfect athlete. It was a pressure I put on myself that wasn't fair. Unfortunately, I see myself placing that same pressure on my daughter. This is a crucial time to remind both her and myself that Jesus doesn't expect perfection. However, He does tell the woman in John 8 to "go, and from now on sin no more." We need to remember that phrase. He doesn't condemn us, but we must choose to follow His guidance. In His broken body, we find healing for our brokenness. In His blood, we find cleansing from the stains of shame we carry.

The following section touches on a sensitive topic: depression and its connection to suicidal thoughts. Though these experiences are deeply personal, I share them with the hope of offering comfort and perspective. If you or someone you know is struggling, please seek professional help. There is always hope, and you are never alone.

During my battle with depression, the shame was overwhelming and dark, feeling impossible to escape. For many men, this shame becomes unbearable, and in those moments, suicide can start to feel like the only way out. I was not immune to these thoughts. There were times when I believed that ending my life was the only way to erase the deep shame etched into my soul by depression.

I vividly remember nights when I longed to drink myself into oblivion. The idea of downing whiskey until I passed out, never to wake again, felt like a release. One night stands out in my memory. It was around midnight, and I was drinking my usual Woodford Reserve, my fourth double dram to be exact. I drank it straight because I loved the burn, it made me feel alive. Lying in bed, tipsy and exhausted, I fell asleep with the hope that I wouldn't wake up. My mind convinced me that if I could just quietly fade away, I wouldn't have to carry the weight anymore, no more guilt, no more disappointment, no more feeling like a burden to my family and those I loved. I believed it was the only way to free myself from the suffocating shame.

It's terrifying how convincing those lies can be when you're deep in the grip of depression. The enemy whispers that your life has no value, that your shame is too great to overcome, and that your loved ones would be better off without you. But that's exactly what they are...lies. I came to realize that suicide is never the answer. Jesus offers a way out of shame, a path to healing and peace. He bore our shame on the cross, and in Him, there is freedom.

Even when we feel worthless, we are deeply loved by Jesus. His love isn't based on how well we perform or how "put together" we appear. In our darkest moments, He is there, extending grace and love to carry us through. I know now that people do love us, even when we can't see it. Our families and friends depend on us as men, on our leadership, our presence, and our love. And as men, we are called to rise above the darkness, not by our own strength, but by the strength we find in Jesus.

If you're reading this and those same dark thoughts have crept into your mind, please know this: you matter. Your life has purpose. Suicide may seem like an escape, but it's a permanent answer to temporary pain. There is always hope, even when it feels impossible to find. Reach out. Let others help. Jesus is ready to lift your burden of shame and replace it with His peace.

At the end of the day, we can't remove our shame on our own. I tried for a long time, convincing myself I was still a "good Christian" if I could just get better. But it wasn't until I surrendered my shame to Jesus that I began to experience true freedom. The truth is, we were never meant to carry the weight of shame, that's why Jesus died for us. His death was the ultimate act of love, and His resurrection is the promise that shame no longer has power over us.

As I close this chapter, I want to remind you: there is a way out. The shame, the guilt, the feeling that you're not enough, they don't have to define you. Jesus already bore it all on the cross. Salvation through Him is the only way to be truly free from shame and to find rest from the battles within.

We were never promised immunity from life's hardships, but we are promised that through Christ, we can find peace even in the storm. He took the shame so we could walk in freedom. And that, my friend, is where true hope lives.

—◦◊◦—

CHAPTER 16

◇◇◇◇◇◇◇◇◇◇◇◇◇◇◇◇◇◇◇◇

Be Sober-Minded,

Be Watchful

When I reflect on my journey with depression, the words of 1 Peter 5:8-11 stand out as a stark warning for all of us: "Your adversary the devil prowls around like a roaring lion, seeking someone to devour." I didn't fully grasp the truth of this until I hit the lowest point in my life, feeling utterly consumed by despair. The devil was prowling, and I was vulnerable prey.

At first, I didn't recognize his attacks for what they were. Depression crept in slowly, and initially, I tried to brush it off. But that's the danger, as I've mentioned before, depression often begins as a whisper before growing into a deafening roar. That's how the enemy operates. He doesn't always strike with obvious blows. Sometimes, it's the subtle lies we begin to believe, the creeping feelings of worthlessness, the shame that weighs heavy on the soul.

Before I knew it, I was trapped, feeling like there was no escape.

The devil wants to devour us, but his approach isn't always direct; often, it's through deception and oppression, convincing us that hope is lost. In my darkest hours, I believed I was beyond saving. I felt I had failed my family, my friends, and God. I was isolated in my mind, exactly where the devil wanted me, alone with my shame.

The enemy seeks to divide us, and depression can make us feel like no one truly understands what we're going through. That's one of his greatest lies. The truth, as Scripture reminds us, is that "the same kinds of suffering are being experienced by your brotherhood throughout the world" (1 Peter 5:9). I wasn't alone, but the devil wanted me to believe I was.

When the enemy attacks and those lies begin to creep in, we must be ready to say, "It is written." We must arm ourselves with the Word of God. I learned this the hard way. For a long time, I didn't fight back; I let the lies fester. I wasn't watchful, nor was I standing firm in my faith. The Word is our weapon, and we must wield it against the enemy's lies.

I remember one night, shared in the previous chapter, when the weight of it all nearly crushed me. I was alone, wrestling with thoughts I never imagined I'd have   thoughts of escaping the pain by drinking myself into oblivion, or worse. But even in that darkness, the Word of God came to mind: "God has not given us a spirit of fear, but of power, and of love, and of a sound mind" (2 Timothy 1:7). I spoke it aloud, and as I did, something began to break.

The enemy doesn't want us to realize the power we have. He wants us trapped in darkness, convinced there's no way out. Now, looking back, I see the devil's intent was to destroy me, but

God had other plans. Though the devil prowls, seeking someone to devour, we have a greater hope in Christ. But to hold onto that hope, we must remain sober-minded and watchful. The enemy is real, and he is always searching for ways to deceive and oppress. Depression comes from the enemy, and he waits to consume us whole.

CHAPTER 17

◇◇◇◇◇◇◇◇◇◇◇◇◇◇◇◇◇◇

In Stillness:

Waiting on the Lord

As I passed the two-year mark in my battle with depression, I found myself in a strange place, still waiting on the Lord for complete healing, yet beginning to sense a real purpose. It has been a journey filled with challenges, doubts, and moments of deep loss. But through it all, I have found hope in knowing I am not alone.

As I shared in a previous chapter, God's presence became a constant reassurance to our omnipresent God who never leaves us. Yet, this was not the end of the road. I am still waiting and believing for full healing from depression. People often say waiting can be a good thing. We're told to wait for the right spouse, the right job, but waiting for depression to lift? That doesn't feel as hopeful. Still, I've learned that God's timing is perfect.

In these long two-plus years of waiting, I've discovered more about myself, my relationship with God, and the world around me than I ever imagined. The lessons were often painful, but the growth has been priceless.

Through the darkness, I found a resilience I never knew I had, a strength that comes from God. Not a reward I earned, but a gift of His grace. Grace that carried me through the hard days while I waited on Him. And by that grace, I now have a platform to share my story and stand alongside men struggling with depression, offering hope and understanding.

One of the most profound lessons I've learned is that I am not alone in this fight. In the beginning, I believed I was completely by myself. The people around us often don't help change that mindset. Depression isolates us, convincing us that we are the only ones struggling with these thoughts and feelings. But the truth is far from that. There is a community of people who understand, who empathize, and who are fighting their own battles alongside us. It's a fight worth fighting because, in the struggle, we find solidarity and hope.

You do have to seek out others who are going through depression, so many suffer in silence. Those around you may not understand. To them, you might be the black sheep, and that's okay. There are others who understand exactly what you're going through. I'm grateful to say that I am one of those people now. I get it. I've been deep in the dark pit of despair. I can be your support, someone who cares and truly understands what you're facing.

I've come to realize that depression isn't just a psychological battle, it's a spiritual one as well. It's the devil's voice whispering lies of worthlessness, despair, and hopelessness. It tempts us to end our lives, to surrender to the darkness. It wants us trapped in that pit forever. But depression is not from God; it comes from the devil himself, from the depths of hell. It seeks to destroy us, robbing us of joy and purpose. The enemy mocks our misery.

Yet we are redeemed by the precious blood of Jesus, and in Him, we find hope and salvation. "Praise the LORD! Oh give thanks to the LORD, for he is good, for his steadfast love endures forever!" (Psalm 106:1, ESV). At the beginning of Psalm 106, we are reminded of our worth in redemption, that no matter how broken we feel, we remain beloved children of God. Jesus' sacrifice on the cross assures us that redemption is always available, no matter how far we have strayed. He is there with us in our darkest moments.

Offering comfort, healing, and restoration, salvation, I have come to understand, is not a one-time event but an ongoing journey of faith and transformation. It means surrendering our brokenness to God and allowing Him to work in and through us. It is about finding joy and fulfillment in His presence, even amid the storms of life. He is our true source, not your spouse, not your children, nor your friends. He is everything and can do anything. The choice of salvation shapes our eternity.

Over the past two years, I have discovered new hobbies and activities that bring me joy and fulfillment through God's guidance. Playing the piano, exploring the works of Chopin, painting, and writing have become channels of expression and healing. God has led me to these gifts, which remind me of His beauty and creativity that persist even in the darkest moments.

As I wait on the Lord for complete healing, I do so with renewed purpose and hope. Though the journey ahead may still hold challenges and uncertainties, I know I am not alone. God is with me, filling my heart with joy. In this waiting, I find comfort in the truth that I am redeemed, deeply loved, and never beyond the reach of His grace.

CHAPTER 18

Embracing the Light:

A Journey Toward Hope

As I sit down to write these final words, I am overwhelmed with gratitude and awe at the journey I've traveled. It has been a road marked by valleys of despair and peaks of hope, with twists and turns I could never have predicted. Yet through it all, one constant has remained: my God. As I shared in earlier chapters, my faith was hidden away during the early stages of my depression, but when I realized again that God is for me, it became my anchor. Today, as I write these lines, I celebrate a significant milestone in my battle against depression, my sobriety. Choosing clarity over chaos, strength over surrender.

Admitting I was an alcoholic is still difficult; I've never truly said it out loud to friends or family. But I have stopped staring down the bottom of the whiskey bottle. This victory stands as a testament to resilience and the unwavering support of a Higher Power. I won't deny the journey has been hard. There were moments when the darkness threatened to overwhelm me, when it felt like my spirit might be crushed forever. Yet through it all, I found my faith again and held onto it like a lifeline, trusting that even the darkest nights will give way to dawn.

Choosing sobriety was a pivotal moment in my healing. It was a conscious decision to confront my demons head-on and refuse to let them control my life any longer. I was drinking to quiet the enemy in my mind, the depression that weighed me down and which I thought only alcohol could suppress before recovery. While the road to healing is long and winding, every sober day reflects my strength and determination.

But sobriety alone is not the answer, it's only one piece of the puzzle. Alongside this commitment, I've plunged deeper into my faith than ever before. I've immersed myself in God's truth and the Word, drawing strength, peace, and freedom from its timeless wisdom. Once again, it has become my anchor, guiding me through the stormy seas of self-doubt, depression, and despair.

To those caught in the grip of depression, I offer these words of encouragement: You are not alone. I know what it feels like to believe you are. Even in your darkest moments, there is hope, hope that can give you the strength to face one more day. I get it. I truly get it. There were nights when I sat on the couch in a dark living room, staring out through the floor-to-ceiling windows, watching the stoplights change, wondering if the world would go on without me. Could I end my life right now?

I wish I had fought harder against those false thoughts that no one loved me. I wish I had reached out earlier during my depression. I regret the way I first reached out, through Facebook, to everyone. There are many things I wish I could take back, but

I must trust God to redeem them. So please, reach out. Lean on those who love you, and never underestimate the power of faith to light even the darkest paths.

I never gave in to suicide because of Jesus, but I know that thought crosses many minds during depression, especially for men like me, in their 40s and beyond. So please, talk to someone. Share your darkness. And to those who watch from the sidelines as loved ones battle unseen demons, I urge you to stand in the gap. Be the one they can turn to. Be the light that keeps them alive. Be a beacon of hope in their darkness, a source of strength and support when they have none left to give.

Your love and compassion can be the difference between an attempted suicide and death by suicide. Your love and compassion can pull someone from the grip of depression. Your love and compassion can make all the difference in the world.

As I close this chapter, I stand on the threshold of a new journey. The road ahead may be uncertain, but I walk it with confidence, knowing I am not alone. As long as there are souls shrouded in darkness, I will stand in the gap, praying for their deliverance, just as I wish someone had prayed for me. I chose to live in silence for too long. May the light of hope shine brightly in your heart, guiding you out of the darkness and into the warm embrace of healing and redemption. And may we all find the courage to walk boldly in the light, knowing that with faith as our compass, we can weather any storm that comes our way.

AFTERWORD

As you've followed my journey, I hope you've seen not only the depths of my struggle but also the undeniable grace of God that carried me through. My story isn't just about the pain and darkness of depression, it's about the hope, light, and salvation found only through Jesus Christ. The only way I found freedom from the pit I was trapped in was by surrendering my life to God. It wasn't easy, but it was the only way out. Depression had stripped me of my strength, yet in my weakness, God's power became real to me.

At the heart of my healing was the realization that I couldn't save myself. I needed something greater, someone greater. Jesus Christ came into this world to offer salvation, to rescue us from sin, and to give us eternal life. As the Bible says, "For by grace you have been saved through faith. And this is not your own doing; it is the gift of God, not a result of works, so that no one may boast" (Ephesians 2:8-9, ESV).

Salvation isn't earned; it's a gift received. If you're reading this and have never asked Jesus to be Lord of your life, I invite you to do so now. God's grace is sufficient for you, just as it was for me. You don't have to fight your battles alone anymore.

Here is a simple prayer you can say:

Lord Jesus, I know I am a sinner, and I ask for Your forgiveness. I believe You died for my sins and rose from the dead. I turn from my sins and invite You into my heart and life. I want to trust and follow You as my Lord and Savior. Amen.

If you prayed that prayer sincerely, welcome to the family!

Today, I can say I am over two years sober, 804 days, to be exact, and hopefully many more to come. By the grace of God, I have found peace and purpose. It wasn't an overnight transformation, but God was faithful every step of the way.

As you close this book and move forward in your own life, remember this: God is in control. Even when you don't feel it or see it, He is working all things together for your good. Trust in His power. There is hope, healing, and freedom in Him.

Believe in His love and never forget: He is always with you.

Be well, and may God bless you on your journey.

—◦◊◦—

AUTHOR BIO

Ryan Foster is a husband, father, and follower of Jesus who writes from the intersection of faith, mental health, and real life. Having walked through depression, shame, and seasons of deep spiritual struggle, Ryan shares his story not as someone who has it all figured out, but as someone who has learned to trust God in the waiting.

He is married to his wife, Kerri, and together they are raising their daughter, Adeline. Ryan also hosts the Rebuilt with Ryan podcast, where he explores marriage, family, and mental health through a Christ-centered lens.

Through his writing, Ryan hopes to remind others that even in the darkest moments, God is near, His promises are sure, and healing, though often slow, is always possible.

www.ingramcontent.com/pod-product-compliance
Lightning Source LLC
Chambersburg PA
CBHW071438130726

47997CB00006B/2145